Marian Keyes

Saved by Cake

photography by Alistair Richardson

MICHAEL JOSEPH
an imprint of
PENGUIN BOOKS

MICHAEL JOSEPH

Published by the Penguin Group

Penguin Books Ltd
80 Strand, London WC2R ORL, England

Penguin Group (USA) Inc.
375 Hudson Street, New York, New York 10014, USA

Penguin Group (Canada)
90 Eglinton Avenue East, Suite 700, Toronto,
Ontario, Canada M4P 2YR
(a division of Pearson Penguin Canada Inc.)

Penguin Ireland
25 St Stephen's Green, Dublin 2, Ireland
(a division of Penguin Books Ltd)

Penguin Group (Australia)
250 Camberwell Road, Camberwell,
Victoria 3124, Australia
(a division of Pearson Australia Group Pty Ltd)

Penguin Books India Pvt Ltd
11 Community Centre, Panchsheel Park,
New Delhi – 110 017, India

Penguin Group (NZ)
67 Apollo Drive, Rosedale, Auckland 0632,
New Zealand (a division of Pearson New Zealand

Penguin Books (South Africa) (Pty) Ltd
24 Sturdee Avenue,Rosebank, Johannesburg 2196,
South Africa

Penguin Books Ltd, Registered Offices: 80 Strand,
London WC2R ORL, England

www.penguin.com

First published 2012
1

Set in BentonModDisp, Filosofia, Bell MT Std,
Rosewood and Nelly Script

Printed in Germany by Mohn Media
Colour reproduction by Altaimage Ltd

A CIP catalogue record for this book is available from
the British Library

ISBN: 978-0-718-15889-7

Saved by Cake

Contents

For Himself, with all my love

Introduction

Medically speaking, there is no such thing as a nervous breakdown. Which is very annoying to discover when you're right in the middle of one.

Mind you, I didn't know I was having one until I was about 6 months into it. It started in October 2009, when panic started rolling up from my gut and down from my head and pushing out from behind my eyes. I felt like I was dreaming, like I'd woken up in the middle of a horrible nightmare, only to discover that I'd been awake all along. Too much reality was rushing in through my eyes. I felt desperate and terrified without knowing why, while I was afraid to tell anyone how I felt because I knew they'd tell me there was nothing to be afraid of and I knew that that wouldn't make the fear go away. I put all my energy into acting 'normal', but I felt like I was driving a car where the controls were no longer working. Crowds terrified me, people zoomed at me, their words rained down on me like electric sparks and my mouth wouldn't work to produce the right response.

I was in the middle of promoting a novel and I thought it must be the stress of that, perhaps an overload of adrenaline, but when the book promotion came to an end, I plunged far deeper into the awful, alien strangeness. It was time for me to start writing again – I'd started a book a couple of months before and it was waiting for me to continue with it – but I didn't know how. I couldn't manage to make an off-the-cuff remark about the weather, never mind write a novel.

I went away on holiday, to a beautiful tropical place, and at the risk of sounding disgustingly ungrateful, I felt like I was in hell. The sea, the sky, the sun, it all looked sinister and strange. I was afraid to be anywhere. I desperately wanted to go home. Even when I was at home. I hardly recognized where I lived. I barely recognized my husband, my mother, my own face. I wondered if I was dead – if I'd accidentally managed to die without noticing it – and was in hell.

I was diagnosed with depression, but it didn't feel like depression. Granted, I had lots of the symptoms: I couldn't sleep; I couldn't breathe; I couldn't eat; I couldn't read – by the time I came to the end of a sentence, I'd forgotten the start. Time had slowed down and each second took an eternity to tick by. Everything looked ugly and pointy and scary, even babies and flowers and Mulberry bags.

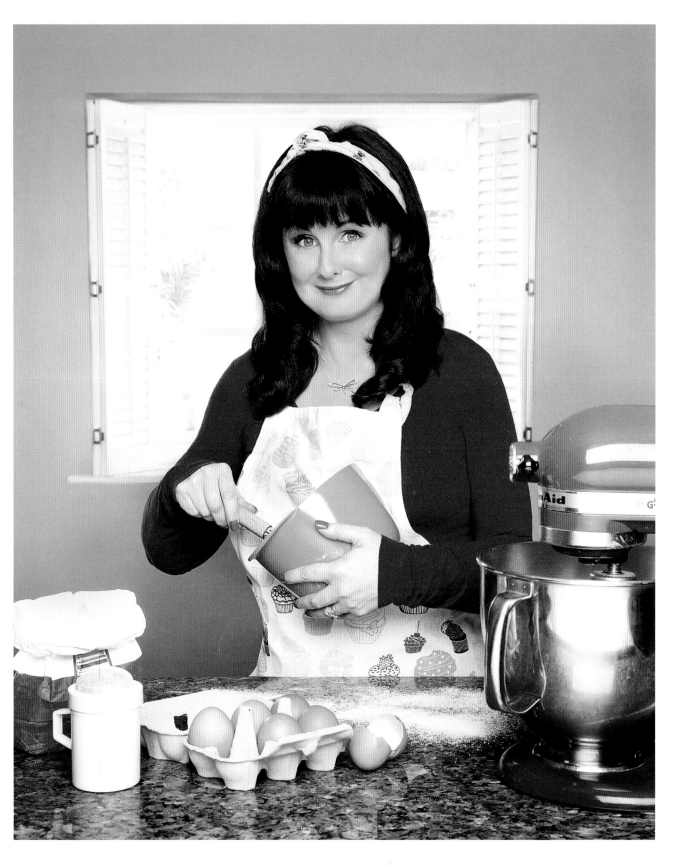

But I didn't feel depressed; what I felt was very, very afraid. I felt like I'd been poisoned, like my brain had been poisoned. I felt like there had been an avalanche in my head and I'd been shunted along by some awful force, to some strange place, off the map, where there was nothing I recognized and no one familiar. I was totally lost.

Some people will look at the outside of my life and see that I want for nothing and say that I'm just feeling sorry for myself, and that's their prerogative. Some people don't understand and will never understand and I envy them. But the brain or the psyche or whatever we should call it is a delicate and difficult-to-understand thing. Whatever was – is – happening to me has nothing to do with my circumstances.

The best way to describe it is I feel like I'm in a science-fiction movie. I feel like I'm living in a parallel universe. I'm on a planet that looks very similar to Earth, but it pulses with a totally different energy, something malign and threatening. The people I know and love have been replaced with sinister doppelgängers and I feel like I'll never get back home. The way back has closed and disappeared and I'm trapped here in this awful, unfamiliar place.

I've tried curing myself in countless different ways. I took – take – a variety of antidepressants, I spent time in a psychiatric hospital – I thought it might be a sanctuary, literally an asylum – but everywhere I went, I took myself with me. I've tried Cognitive Behavioural Therapy, acupuncture, reiki, meditation, mindfulness, B12 injections, Bach Flower Remedies, journaling, ice-cold showers – anything that was recommended, I gave it a go. I tried exercising, but it seemed such a brutal thing to do to my terribly fragile self. I tried yoga, but I couldn't be alone in my own head. I tried spending time with friends, but that terrified me because I didn't recognize them. I tried focusing on other people, on any way I could help, but got knocked back at every attempt – I tried to volunteer for various charities, but was defeated by their complicated, lengthy application forms. I went to donate blood and they told me to hop it because I'd lived in the UK during the mad cow drama. I asked if anyone needed their living room painted, but no one did.

I begged people to let me drive them places. Driving was the one skill I could still manage. I knew I was disconnected from the world, so I drove with extra care. Sometimes I stopped at bus stops and offered to take people wherever they wanted to go, but no one would ever get in with me. Not – I think – because they saw I was mad, but because no one gets into cars with strangers.

Friends and family allowed me to give them lifts and I thanked them over and over. My previous self never had enough time to do such things; now I had endless, endless days and hours and minutes to fill. The old me used to speed up at amber lights; now I slowed down, grateful to legitimately kill a few seconds at a red light. I kept trying to write. I made a contract with myself that I'd do an hour a day, even if I just sat in front of the computer and stared at the screen, but I couldn't manage even that.

I thought a lot about dying. I had a 'suicide bag' that included, among other things, sheets of A4 paper, Sellotape and big markers. These were to write big warning signs to be stuck to the door of the hotel bathroom, warning the chambermaid not to come in. I didn't want her traumatized. 'STOP!' The notes said. 'DON'T COME IN! I HAVE KILLED MYSELF. CALL THE GUARDS.' (I'd decided, after lots of deliberating, that it would be better to kill myself at a hotel. I even had the right one picked out – a grim concrete block. I'd always thought it was the sort of place you'd go to if you wanted to kill yourself. I felt that if I did it at home, the house would be poisoned forever for Himself. That's the kind of logic my brain was presenting myself with.)

But though I hovered – and still hover – on the brink of suicide, I did feel enough of a sense of responsibility to the people who loved me not to go through with it. Whatever was going on with me, I had to wait it out. I had to find ways of passing the time until I was restored to myself again.

Then, one day, my friend Helen Cosgrove was visiting. Her birthday was coming up and all of a sudden I decided I wanted to bake Helen a birthday cake. I hadn't baked in decades, not since myself and my classmates had been forced to assemble some joyless rock cakes in Home Economics when we were thirteen. To be honest, I didn't really hold with baking. I was suspicious of anything 'crafty'. The resurgence in knitting and needlepoint and suchlike, I thought it was a bit of an affectation. And who had the time to bake? Why would you spend time and effort making something yourself when you could just go out and buy something far nicer in Marks & Spencers? I'd secretly mocked any person who had ever engaged with a piping bag.

But things were different now. So I baked Helen a cake – a chocolate cheesecake, as it happens. And I enjoyed making it so much that I baked another. And another. I started reading recipe books and looking up stuff on the internet. I investigated the science of baking and I went on a couple of courses (nothing too challenging, but enough for me to get the basics).

I couldn't stop baking. And although I consumed a truly heroic quantity of my produce, I couldn't eat it all and eventually had to start giving it away – to family members, neighbours, random strangers. At first people were charmed. Then a little overwhelmed. Eventually when they saw me coming, baked goods in hand, they started jumping behind walls or tried to disguise themselves as convection heaters. And still I kept – and keep on – baking.

I need to make something clear: baking may not be for you and if it isn't, I'm sorry and I hope you find something that helps. I also need to tell you that baking hasn't 'cured' me. But it gets me through. My challenge – everyone's challenge – is about living through today and I find that baking passes the time. To be perfectly blunt about it, my choice sometimes is: I can kill myself or I can make a dozen cupcakes. Right so, I'll do the cupcakes and I can kill myself tomorrow.

Baking makes me concentrate on what's right in front of my nose. I have to focus. On weighing the sugar. On sieving the flour. I find it calming and rewarding because, in fairness, it is sort of magic – you start off with all this disparate stuff, like butter and eggs, and what you end up with is so totally different. And also delicious.

The thing is that I was absolutely clueless. I was a total beginner and I had to learn everything. I've taught myself to bake by doing it over and over again and while I'm not claiming to be any sort of expert – I've made tons and tons of mistakes along with tons and tons of cakes – I've learnt the basics and all kinds of handy little helpful tips and am delighted to share them with you.

Funnily enough, the part I enjoy most is the decorating. I say 'funnily' because all my life I was famed in my family for being 'bad with my hands'. I was always terrible at drawing and sewing and I hated wrapping presents – I hadn't the patience to cut the paper neatly or tear off the right amount of Sellotape. But it turns out that I can ice a cake. I've learnt how to – would you believe! – use a piping bag and I've become a dab hand in nozzle work.

But don't be alarmed, no one is going to make you do nozzle work; this is a book about baking. I've included my favourite recipes. Some are very straight-forward and simple because that was all I could handle at the time. And some are more complex – for example, the Banana Meringue Pie (see page 147) involves baking pastry, making a custard and making the meringue – because there were times when I needed a challenge, when I needed to concentrate hard.

Either way, I can promise you that they're all delicious and I hope that you get some pleasure from making them. And indeed eating them.

Equipment List

I didn't own a single baking accoutrement the day the urge to bake came 'at' me, literally not a thing. I had to get in my car and drive to the local supermarket (I had no idea that specialist cake equipment shops existed back then) and buy a couple of basic sandwich tins, along with the ingredients. Since then I've discovered that there's a whole universe of baking tools out there and I've acquired stuff on an as-needed basis. To be honest it feels like the more I get, the more I want, but I'm like that about everything. Once I start buying into a need, any need, it kick-starts some bottomless, insatiable black hole in me.

Don't get me started on cookie cutters. I'd been alive on the planet for several decades without ever knowing they even existed until one day I happened to be in a bake shop and saw an adorable little metal thing in the shape of a handbag. I was charmed beyond belief, and purchased it with alacrity, warm with love and certain that it was the only cookie cutter I would ever need in my whole life. This state of satisfied bliss lasted approximately 7 seconds. Then I saw a cutter in the shape of a shoe and was felled with a terrible agony of want, so I got that one too. Briefly the beast was quieted. Then my appalling, needy eyes alighted on a quartet of stars, sized from dinky to large, and the longing started all over again. Since then I've gone on to acquire cookie cutters in the shape of cars, hearts, circles, flowers, fairy wings, stars, owls, moose, bats, beer mugs, football boots, rabid dogs, gangrenous legs, rotten teeth … and still I want more. If I had every cookie cutter in the world, it still wouldn't be enough.

Anyway, I digress. Here is a list of the most basic equipment you'll need:

Mixing bowl

Whatever kind you like. Those old-fashioned beige ceramic ones keep your ingredients cold so are good for doing pastry. Also, they have a certain stern retro air, a certain 'I know what I'm doing' look to them, which can work well to intimidate guests to your kitchen. For myself, I have a blue plastic bowl.

Electric mixer

In the beginning, I managed fine with the cheapest possible hand-held one, but after a certain mileage, the motor burnt out on me. (In fairness, I was making cakes around the clock. I was like a wartime munitions factory and no machine could have withstood my frenzied demands.) Obviously, the more you pay, the more functions and stuff you get, all the way up to the gadget du jour, a KitchenAid. 'An extra pair of hands', to quote their marketing. (No, I didn't get a free one from them. I haven't got free anything from anyone. If I recommend anything, it's only because I think it's good.)

Sieve

For getting the lumps out of flour or icing sugar. Also – this came as a surprise to me – to add air to the mix, thus ensuring light and fluffy cakes.

Cake tins

Springform ones are lovely and handy for getting the cakes out without sticking. Also, silicone moulds work great and are, of course, modern, space age and exciting. (Remember to put them on a baking tray before you add the cake mixture because otherwise they'll flop all over the place and spill everything.) If you're wondering which width tin to start with, 20cm is probably the most used size. Get two. Also, something that I find I use incessantly is a 20cm by 20cm square tin.

Pie dishes

If you're planning on making pastry, it would be no harm to get a pie dish – it can be metal or ceramic, and is very similar to a cake tin, except that the edges slope outwards. A width of 20cm or 22cm should cover most eventualities. An extra complication is that pie dishes come in different depths. I'd recommend that your first purchase be a 'shallow' one, which is about 3cm deep. And in the fullness of time you might get yourself a 'deep' one, which has a depth of 5cm.

Cupcake tray

To 'hold' your paper cases because, left to its own devices, cake mix will push against the folds in the paper, will spread like wildfire and you'll end up with pancakes rather than cupcakes.

Purple silicone spatula

If you can't get purple, I suppose another colour would do. This device is so brilliant at scraping your bowl, you'll probably get an extra half cake out of the mix. Sadly though, it means there's less left to lick. Or is that such a bad thing? One of the few downsides of being a keen baker is 'getting high on your own supply'. I'd somehow convinced myself, as I shovelled raw cake into my mouth, that if it wasn't cooked, it didn't count. I was wrong.

Palette knife

You may not need this as such, but if you're anything like me, you'll really enjoy it. I adore my palette knife. I love its beautiful strength and flexibility and sometimes I nip into the kitchen and spend a few happy minutes bending it backwards and forwards, cocking my ear for the faint but beautiful 'whop-whop' noise it makes. It's almost a hobby in itself, like bursting bubble wrap.

Baking paper

Important fact – greaseproof paper is NOT the same as baking paper. No. Greaseproof paper is a ho-hum product that was used to line cake tins back in the olden days, but often failed in its job and stuck to cakes, stuck to tins and often made a hash of things. Baking paper, on the other hand, is newfangled magical stuff because it's made with silicone and never sticks to anything.

Apron

Okay, maybe it's not vital, but it's a laugh.

Wire cooling rack

It lets hot air evaporate from your just-baked cakes, so that they don't end up continuing to cook in their own steam.

Digital weighing scales

Not as expensive as it sounds – don't let the word 'digital' alarm you. But accuracy is important in baking. They say cooking is an art and baking is a science. Chemical reactions happen during baking and it's actually a very delicate business.

Airtight tin

All a bit Cath Kidston and retro, I know, but you want your stuff to stay fresh. The smaller stuff lasts the shortest amount of time. Make sure your baked goods are fully cooled before you put them into the airtight tin because the heat and the anaerobic atmosphere will mean germs will be having the time of their life in there, dancing, riding and procreating at a ferocious rate, otherwise.

Basic icing kit

Icing is a whole universe in itself and to go into detail about it would fill at least a whole other book. But if you'd like to be able to have a little bit of fun and do basic swirls and stars and suchlike on top of cupcakes, why not treat yourself to a little beginners' kit. There are lots on the market, all containing a selection of differently shaped nozzles, some piping bags and an instruction booklet. Wilton's do a good one, but I'm sure most other brands are fine as well. Also, there is no shame at all in using pre-made Writing Icing – I use Dr. Oetker's all the time.

Sugar paste gun

I'm joking. I mean you can if you want, but you'd want to be in a bad way, obsession-wise.

Some Rules

Only a few, but they'll help.

1. **Don't be afraid.** Really. It's only cake. Even if it's a disaster – and there will be times when despite you doing everything perfectly it will be – it's not the end of the world. While it's vital to follow recipes, we must remember we're still dealing with organic stuff – flour, butter, fruit and all that; one bag of sugar cannot be guaranteed to behave exactly the same as another. Also every oven is different. Even in the one oven, conditions can be different! (Once you start moving in baking circles you might hear talk of the famed 'Hot Spot', a part of your oven that is inexplicably hotter than all the rest of it.) What I'm trying to say is that sometimes even when you do everything right, things will go wrong. Sometimes bad cakes happen to good people. It is not your fault.

2. **Before you begin making a cake, before you crack a single egg, read the entire recipe** – ingredients, equipment required and oven temperatures – through from start to finish.

3. **For cakes and cupcakes have your eggs, butter and milk at room temperature.** Take them out of the fridge about an hour before you start.

4. **For making pastry, on the other hand, have everything as *cold* as possible** – the ingredients, the bowl and especially your hands. Some people are born with 'hot hands' – genetics have dealt them a marked card. I am one of those misfortunates and well-meaning, chilly-handed types have advised me to give up on pastry and stick to cake. But I've decided to defy the odds, to challenge the limitations I was born with. So yes, I make pastry. It won't be winning any prizes, but I like doing it.

5. **Have your tin lined or greased before you start**, especially if you're dealing with raising agents (e.g. bicarbonate of soda, baking powder or self-raising flour.) When your raising agent comes into contact with liquid (e.g. eggs or milk), a chemical reaction begins and gas is generated but only for a short period of time. You don't want that gas ebbing away into the ether, instead you want that gas inside your cake, raising it and making it light and fluffy. So as soon as you add whatever raising agent you're using, you've got to get the whole business into cake tins and into the oven as quickly as possible.

6. **After you've put your cake in the oven, it is imperative that you don't open the door for as long as possible.** If you're new to baking you might be dying to see how it's all getting on in there. This is natural. A bit like the first time you applied fake tan, perhaps, and had to check every 5 minutes if it was coming up. And when nothing was happening, adding a bit more. Then more. Then ending up madly orange and streaky several hours later. Patience and restraint are what's called for. Resist the urge to open the oven door every 30 seconds. The cold air from outside will rush in and interfere with the raising process and you'll end up with a sunken, miserable cake. A 'flop', quite literally.

7. **Also, if you were planning on having a temper tantrum and doing a lot of stomping and door-slamming in the kitchen region, now might not be the best time.** Cakes are sensitive little flowers and are easily distressed by loud noises. Could you hold off until your cake is done?

8. **Ingredients go funny after a while, even the dry goods; they sort of 'die'.** Baking powder loses its mojo, so does self-raising flour and dried spices turn to a dust of nothingness. There are times when people end up with cakes that are flat and tasteless and they wonder what they've done wrong and maybe they've done nothing wrong, maybe it's just that their ingredients were past it. My suggestion is that if you bake only once a decade, why not treat yourself to a new bag of flour.

Techniques and Helpful Hints

Lining a loaf tin with baking paper

When lining a tin, a technique you might find useful to get the baking paper to stay where you want it to is to cut one piece big enough to cover the base and come right up the sides. Then – yes, I know it sounds strange – crumple it into a small ball and open it out again. Something about being crumpled makes it more pliable and less airy and floaty.

Salted or unsalted butter?

You get your unsalted fundamentalists. Many cake recipes are adamant that only unsalted butter will do, and round where I live, unsalted butter is like a shy woodland creature – an elusive, obscure thing. Sometimes it's in the shop and other times it isn't. You might get lucky, or then again you mightn't, but you can never bank on getting it. In my early days of baking, I thought that if I couldn't get the unsalted stuff, that there was no point at all in using the salted stuff, but it turns out that I'm wrong – salted butter works fine for baking. In fact, I went on to discover that there are as many pro-salted butter advocates as there are unsalted. Experiment. These are your cakes. The choice is yours.

Melting chocolate

Now, about melting chocolate. What you need to know is that it must be done with great caution. A skittish, unpredictable beast is chocolate when it comes to being melted. Burns at the drop of a hat. Also, it does something called 'seizing', which basically means it gathers together in a stubborn, surly ball and can't be coaxed to do anything else, just like a broken-hearted teenager. So you've two choices:

You can melt your chocolate by breaking it into a heatproof bowl and setting the bowl over a saucepan of simmering water. But don't let a single drop of water get on the chocolate, don't even let the bottom of the bowl sit in the water, else things will be seizing left, right and centre.

Or you can melt chocolate by breaking it into pieces and microwaving it, but listen to me: do it in 30-second bursts at half power and stir it between each bout, even when – and I can't stress this enough – *even when it looks exactly the same as the last time you saw it*, 30 seconds previously.

One final note – white chocolate 'suffers with its nerves'. It's even more prone to burning than dark or milk chocolate, so take extra care with it.

Whatever melting method you use, do it slowly.

'Scalding' milk or cream

This means heating it until it's almost boiling, but without actually letting it boil. This involves standing over the hob, staring unblinkingly at the milk, every nerve and sinew strained. Don't feel foolish, this is the only way. When the perfect temperature is achieved, whip the pan off the heat.

Separating eggs

When you have to separate several eggs, a handy trick is to use 3 bowls. This way, if you accidentally spill yolk into your white, or (horrors!) get a bad egg, at least the damage is confined to just one egg and not the whole batch.

Begin by cracking your first egg. Let the white pour into what will henceforth be known as Bowl No. 1 – basically this is an interim bowl, you're simply using it as a middleman. When as much of the white as you can extract is in Bowl No. 1, tip the yolk into Bowl No. 2 (also known at the **Bowl of Shame**, see page 144) Then! Empty the contents of Bowl No. 1 into your third bowl, now known as Bowl No. 3. Start on the next egg. Pour the white into Bowl No. 1, the yolk into the Bowl of Shame, then empty the contents of Bowl No. 1 into Bowl No. 3. And so on.

Banishing egg shell

If you accidentally get some egg shell in your egg white, what you must do is to scoop it out with another piece of egg shell. I know it sounds counterintuitive to be adding even more unwelcome shell, but this really works.

Baking blind

Not, as you might imagine, baking with a bandana around your eyes as if you're about to face a firing squad. No. This is a method of baking a pastry case before the filling goes in. Once the raw pastry is in the tin, line it with a layer of greaseproof paper and weight it down with something. I use dried beans, but you can get gorgeous little glass balls from specialist baking shops. Blind baking achieves two things:

* The pastry under the filling will be cooked and therefore not soggy.

* The weight of the beans (or gorgeous little glass balls) will stop the pastry rising and puffing and generally becoming unsuitable to 'receive' filling.

Making a biscuit base for cheesecake

To crush the biscuits for the base, break them up roughly, put them in a plastic bag and tie a knot in it. Then put that plastic bag in another plastic bag (you'll see why in a minute). Reach for a blunt instrument. I personally favour a mallet, but you can use a hammer, a rolling pin, even a wine bottle, basically anything that can inflict grievous bodily harm.

Belt and bash until the biscuits turn to dust. You'll see now why you need the second plastic bag, because in all the excitement you might accidentally tear the first one and have crumbs all over the kitchen. (Can I just point out that you can save yourself all of this work if you have a food processor, but sometimes it's the journey itself that's enjoyable.)

Getting your cheesecake out of the tin

I've uncovered a conspiracy of silence around this and no recipe ever seems to address it. Here's what I've learnt the hard way. Use a springform tin, but don't spring the catch until the very last moment. By then the lengthy period of refrigeration will have caused the cake to contract slightly and 'pull' away from the sides of its container. Gently slide your palette knife between the tin and cake and methodically work it all the way round. When you feel the cake has been fully loosened from the tin, then – AND ONLY THEN – do you spring the catch. That part of the tin should lift off easily.

So that's the outside done. How do you get the base off? A lot trickier. Do you think the cake looks and feels firm enough to do the 'two-plate' trick? If so, place a big flat plate face downwards on top of the cheesecake. It's important that the plate is flat. If it has an indent, no matter how shallow, it can cause the cake to crack and, Christ knows, no one wants that to happen. Slide one hand under the base of the cheesecake and place the other hand on top of the face-downwards plate so that you're actually sandwiching the cake between your hands. However, now is not the time to start thinking about the terrible responsibility of that. Action is key. Keeping your fingers spread and your hands wide, working quickly, but smoothly, flip the cake over, so that now it's sitting upside down on the plate. The base of the tin will still be attached to it, but using your palette knife, gently, gently, gently ease it off, leaving your lovely biscuit base behind.

Then it's time to turn the cake the right way round. Place a second big flat plate – the plate you want your cake to be sitting on – face downwards on the upside-down cake. Slide one hand underneath the bottom plate and put the other on the top plate and, once again, flip. Voilà! Now you should have your intact cheesecake, sitting on its serving plate, facing the right direction.

Sometimes, when I've taken the springform edging off, I fear my cheesecake looks a little too wobbly and fragile to survive this traumatic two-plate process, and then I think, No, I'll be kind to it, I'll simply serve it on the base of the tin.

Glitter, sprinkles, sparkles and sugar balls, etc.

I get as much pleasure from decorating cakes – particularly cupcakes – as I do from baking them. To ice a cupcake and then to create a piece of edible art on top of it from glitter, sugar flowers, writing gel, fondant stars, etc. is the most wonderful feeling. An ordinary supermarket will have some sprinkles on their shelves, but to get some idea of the universe of decorations available to you, I'd really recommend that you go to a specialist bakeshop or website (www.cakescookiesandcraftsshop.co.uk is divine). You'll be dazzled and amazed and want to buy everything on it. You'll have the most wonderful time, I promise you.

How do you know when your cake is cooked?

Well, it tells you. If you press it gently and it 'replies', i.e. springs back, you're in business. Or you can do the **Skewer Test**. Also known as the Cocktail Stick Test. Basically, what happens is, when the allotted baking time is up, you stick a skewer (or indeed a cocktail stick) into the middle of the cake, then pull it straight back out again. If the skewer has cake mix sticking to it, you're not done yet. But if it comes out clean, the cake is cooked. Huzzah.

CLASSICS

Rock Cakes

Victoria Sandwich

Buttermilk Scones

Rhubarb Crumble

John's Sticky Toffee Pudding

Simple Chocolate Mousse

Himself's Millionaire's Shortbread

Christmas Cake without Fear
(aka Traditional Fruit Cake)

Bread and Butter Pudding

It's not my way to keep things simple. No matter what I'm doing, I get a wild urge to up the ante. But in this section, I'm showing some respect. These recipes have been around for a long time and they've survived because they're so great. I remember lots of them from my childhood, and making any of these is a great way to start baking or to reintroduce yourself to baking if you've been away from it for a while.

Rock Cakes

Rock Cakes. Well, when I was growing up, they were considered a bit of a joke. The fault was definitely in the name – a cake that advertised itself as similar to a rock had to be hard and joyless, right? I made them countless times in Home Economics – oddly, they're the only things I actually can remember baking in that class – but I've no memory of what they tasted like. I don't think I even bothered to eat them. At the time I was obsessed with Yorkies and I had no interest in any kind of sweetmeat that wasn't shop bought.

However, I believe Rock Cakes have recently undergone a radical image makeover and are in big demand at children's birthday parties, thanks to Harry Potter being a fan of them. And now it transpires that the 'Rock' of the title doesn't refer to the inedible hardness of the cakes, but the fact that they look like rocks. With this in mind, I recently remade them and what a surprise! They're lovely. Sweet and crumbly and nothing like rocks! The key, according to my mother-in-law Shirley, is to eat them pretty much as soon as they're baked.

Makes 14–16

225g self-raising flour
1 teaspoon baking powder
115g butter
115g sultanas
50g mixed peel
75g caster sugar
1 egg, beaten
3 tablespoons milk

To decorate
3 tablespoons demerara sugar

Line a large baking tray with baking paper and preheat the oven to 200°C/400°F/gas 6.

Sieve the flour and baking powder into a large bowl, then rub in the butter until it resembles breadcrumbs (or get your machine to do it). Stir in the sultanas, mixed peel, sugar and the beaten egg, mixing well together, until you have a stiff dough. If it's too stiff, add milk by the tablespoon, remembering you can always add more if you need it but it's a lot harder to take out if you've added too much.

Using 2 tablespoons – one for scooping, the other for scooping off (if you get me) – place golf ball-sized mounds of the mixture on to the prepared baking tray, leaving space for spreading between each one. Do not worry yourself about making these boyos look smooth – remember they're meant to look craggy. The clue is in the name.

Sprinkle the top of each little mound with demerara sugar, then bake for 15 to 20 minutes until the cakes have gone golden brown. Cool on a wire rack and eat before too long. Gadzooks, or By Gor, or whatever it is that Harry Potter says.

Victoria Sandwich

This delightfully light sponge is as traditional as it gets and extremely easy to make. I've used strawberry jam and fresh cream to sandwich the two layers together, but you could use anything really. Lemon curd and Greek yoghurt, for example. Or raspberry syrup and buttercream icing. Or Nutella and chocolate shavings. Right, I'll stop now.

Makes 8 slices

For the cake
200g butter
200g caster sugar
4 eggs
the seeds of 1 vanilla pod or 1 teaspoon vanilla extract
200g self-raising flour

To decorate
200ml whipping cream
200g strawberry jam
4 tablespoons icing sugar

Butter two 20cm tins and line the bases with baking paper. Preheat the oven to 190°C/375°F/gas 5.

Cream the butter and sugar together until pale and fluffy. Add the eggs, one by one, beating between each addition. The mix might curdle a little. Don't be alarmed. Simply add a tablespoon or two of flour and it should be okay. Stir in the vanilla seeds (see page 56 on how to de-seed a vanilla pod) or extract. Sieve in the flour and fold through.

Divide the mix between the two tins and bake for about 20 minutes, until your skewer comes out clean or the cake bounces back at you when you press it gently. Cool on a wire rack and remove from their tins. When the cakes are fully cooled, whip the cream until stiff, almost buttery.

Place one cake on a serving plate (could you get your hands on a paper doily? This retro cake simply cries out for a doily!). Cover the surface of the cake with a layer of the strawberry jam, then a layer of the cream. Place the second cake on top. The jam and cream might squish slightly out of the sides, so use a knife to scrape off the excess. Using a sieve, sprinkle icing sugar over the surface of the cake. Because this recipe uses fresh cream, don't hang about too long before serving it.

Buttermilk Scones

I grew up watching a legion of Irish Mammies effortlessly making the most wonderful scones. They just flung flour and other stuff into a bowl – they never seemed to weigh or measure anything. Casually, while simultaneously doing several other things, they'd produce a lump of dough, throw it on to a floured surface and, with dizzying speed, stamp out several perfect rounds. Into the oven with them and 10 to 12 minutes later, we'd have a houseful of amazingly delicious scones. They made it look so easy that I thought it was.

But no, my amigos, it can be quite tricky. My first attempts were disastrous in so many ways – too flat, too biscuity, too cracked, too lopsided and just way, way too strange-looking. So I've gone back to the source – the Irish Mammy – and garnered some of their secrets, which I'm happy to share with you.

The thing everyone was agreed on was that the oven must be very hot – 220°C. If you manage to set off the smoke alarm, things are looking good. Before you start cutting out the scones, the dough needs to be patted flat and smooth – any small cracks in the surface of the uncooked dough will become gaping canyons once they're cooked. Also, the dough must be quite tall – about 5cm – so that the scones will be high and 'crumby' and not flat and 'biscuity'. Finally, when you're taking the cutter out of the dough, don't twist it. I know it's almost irresistible, but it will definitely result in a lopsided scone.

Makes 13–15 scones

265g plain flour

½ teaspoon baking powder

½ teaspoon bicarbonate of soda

65g caster sugar

¾ teaspoon salt

130g butter, at room temperature

110–165ml buttermilk, plus extra for washing the tops of the scones

Preheat the oven to 220°C/425°F/gas 7 and line two baking trays with baking paper. Sieve the flour, baking powder and bicarbonate of soda into a bowl. Add the sugar and salt and mix well. Cut the butter into soft chunks, then 'cut' it into the dry ingredients with a knife until the mixture resembles dry breadcrumbs.

Add enough of the buttermilk to make a soft, not sticky dough, stir well, and move things up a gear. At this stage you need to start working fast. Whatever chemical jiggery-pokery goes on in scones has already started – it began the nanosecond the buttermilk hit the flour, and the 'rising' is already underway. At this stage you can use your hands to bring the dough together. Scatter your work surface with flour. Take about half of the dough out of the bowl, place it on the floured surface, shape it into a lump about 5cm thick and use your hands to pat the surface smooth.

Dip a 5cm scone cutter in flour, plunge it confidently into the dough, cut out a scone and lift the cutter out again. Using a palette knife, lift the scone on to the waiting baking tray. Dip the cutter in flour again, cut a scone, lift it out and keep cutting scones in this fashion until all the dough is used up. Remove the remaining half of the dough from the bowl, scatter the work surface with fresh flour and repeat the entire exercise.

When all the dough is used, pour a small amount of buttermilk in a bowl and use a pastry brush to wash it over the tops of the scones. Bake for about 15 minutes, until they've risen and gone a golden brown. Leave to cool slightly on a wire rack. Serve hot or cold with jam and clotted cream or butter and Cheddar cheese.

Rhubarb Crumble

This is a pure delight to make because it's so quick and easy – you don't have to pre-cook the rhubarb, you just fling everything into the dish and it all cooks together, fruit and topping.

However, it kills me to keep things simple, it really does. I can't *bear* that this isn't Rhubarb, Lychee and Star Fruit crumble. Or Rhubarb, Kiwi and Greengage Crumble. But I made a promise to you at the beginning of this section that I'd keep things classic and really I'm trying my best. Nevertheless, I've taken the small liberty of suggesting sprinkling a tiny teaspoon of dried ginger over the rhubarb because it brings out the flavour. And I've wondered if we might add some porridge oats into the crumble topping, because oats are so good for us and they make the topping extra crunchy. But if you are a crumble purist and I've offended you with my audacity, then, of course, omit the dried ginger, substitute 100g of plain flour for the oats, and we will never refer to the matter again.

Serves 6–8

For the fruit base
900g rhubarb
50g demerara sugar
1 teaspoon ground ginger

For the crumble topping
175g plain flour
50g caster sugar
50g dark muscovado sugar
100g butter, chilled and
  cut into cubes
100g porridge oats

Preheat the oven to 200°C/400°F/gas 6.

Wash and trim the rhubarb stalks, slicing any that are particularly thick in half lengthways first, then cut into chunks about 2.5cm long and toss them in a bowl with the sugar and ginger, if you're using it. Empty the fruit layer ingredients into a 1.5 litre pie dish (no need to grease) and press down.

For the topping, sieve the flour into a bowl, then add the sugars and cold butter cubes (it is vitally important that the butter is cold because if it isn't we'll end up making more of a pastry than a crumble). If you're using a food processor, pulse on short bursts and keep a close eye on things. If you're rubbing in by hand, keep at it until the mix starts to look like a crumble. Add the oats, mix well and sprinkle over the rhubarb mixture, making sure all the fruit is well covered.

Bake for 40 to 45 minutes or until the topping is golden brown. Serve warm, with custard or vanilla ice cream.

John's Sticky Toffee Pudding

So I said to Himself, 'How do you make Sticky Toffee Pudding?' And he said, 'I haven't a clue,' and I said, 'Well, that's very strange, seeing as it's your favourite dessert,' and he said, 'It's not my favourite dessert, I don't have a favourite dessert, I don't really like desserts at all,' so I said, 'Well, *who's* favourite dessert is it then?' And he said, 'My Dad's.' Then he said, 'You're always doing this, mixing me up with my Dad.' And I gave him a saucy look and said, 'Well, *not always.*'

Anyway! I consulted Himself's Dad (whose name is John, a lovely, lovely man) and he gave me this wonderful recipe. It was fascinating to me because, although I've had Sticky Toffee Pudding many times, I'd never really focused on what's in it. Like, who knew about the dates? And the Horlicks? Although John says you can leave the Horlicks out if you like. It gives a tiny hint of malt, but if that's not for you, just skip it. I have to say though, that this pudding (or cake, which is what this really is) is all about the toffee sauce. When you make the sauce you might think you've much too much. Believe me, you haven't.

Finally, just for a bit of fun, I've recommended an optional garnish. Do you know those really, really hard toffee-flavoured sucky sweets? I think they're called Werther's Originals. The ones I found described themselves as 'butter candies'. Well, unwrap fourteen or fifteen of them and put them in a small plastic bag. Put that small plastic bag inside another small plastic bag, tie a knot in the bag, then take a big mallet and bash the living daylights out of the sweets until they're reduced to small shards of delicious toffee-flavoured dust. Sprinkle over the pudding and sauce just before serving.

Serves 9

For the pudding
200g medjool dates
  (the weight after the
  stones have been removed)
1 teaspoon bicarbonate of soda
60g butter
60g caster sugar
2 eggs
1 heaped tablespoon Horlicks
1 teaspoon vanilla extract
150g self-raising flour

For the toffee sauce
175g butter
175g light muscovado sugar
210ml double cream

To decorate (optional)
14 or 15 butter candies, bashed
  to smithereens

Butter a 20cm square tin and preheat the oven to 180°C/350°F/gas 4. Stone the dates if necessary, then chop them roughly. Put them in a bowl with the bicarbonate of soda and cover with 200ml boiling water. Leave to stand for 10 minutes to soften, then drain away the water and whizz the dates in a food processor until they form a purée.

Meanwhile, cream the butter and sugar until pale. Add the eggs, Horlicks and vanilla extract. Sieve in the flour, then fold in the puréed dates. Pour the mix into the prepared tin.

Bake for about 30 to 35 minutes. When the cake is done it will look – perhaps alarmingly – flat. Please don't fret. Remember what I said about this being all about the sauce. Put the tin on a wire rack.

While the cake/pudding is cooling, make the toffee sauce by putting the butter, sugar and cream into a heavy-bottomed saucepan over a low heat until the sugar has dissolved and the butter has melted. Increase the heat a little and stir constantly. After a while, perhaps 10 minutes, the sauce will thicken and darken in colour.

By now it should be possible to take the cake out of the tin without burning the hands off yourself. Cut into nine equal-sized squares and drown them in sauce. Sprinkle with crushed candies.

Simple Chocolate Mousse

This is gorgeous. Beautiful texture. Light, airy and – yes! – moussey.

**Makes 4 large or
6 medium servings**

200g dark chocolate
  (70% cocoa solids)
4 eggs, separated
2 tablespoons caster sugar
225ml whipping cream

To decorate (optional)
squirty cream from a can
chocolate vermicelli

Melt the chocolate using your preferred method (see page 20). Let it cool a little, then whisk in one of the egg yolks. When you feel it's fully absorbed, whisk in the next and so on until they're all in. There's a chance that the mix might go a bit 'congealy'. If you feel it's too thick, add a tablespoon of water. Even two.

In a separate bowl, whisk the 4 egg whites until they start forming soft peaks. Add the sugar and keep whisking until stiff peaks form. In yet another bowl, beat the cream until soft peaks (yes, more peaks) form. Add a third of the chocolate/yolky mix to the cream and mix well. Add another third, beat well, then add the final third. Then, using a big metal spoon, fold the egg whites into the cream/chocolate mix, trying to mix well while 'keeping' the air (a next-to-impossible task if you ask me, but let's try our best).

Divide the mousse into four or six glasses. I'm just talking about ordinary drinking glasses. I used ones with 400ml capacity, but you can use smaller ones, or indeed bigger ones – imagine a pint of chocolate mousse, God, what a beautiful thought! Or, of course, you can use bowls. The good thing about using glasses is that you get to see the mousse before you eat it, which adds to the thrill, I think.

However! Yes, I'm afraid that there *is* a however – for every credit there is a debit – and the downside of using glasses is that the mousse spills down the sides of the glasses, both inside and outside, and the mess has to be cleared up. Amigos, I spent *hours*, and the best part of an entire roll of kitchen paper, carefully wiping the glasses so that they would be fit to present to my expected guests. (Actually, I had no expected guests. I live in an imaginary world and I planned to eat all four mousses myself.) I think I could have made things easier for myself if I'd used differently shaped glasses, ones that were wider at the brim than they were at the base. Like I keep saying, I make the mistakes so that you don't have to.

Chill for at least 3 hours. Decorate, if you like, with a squirt of cream from a can and a sprinkle of chocolate vermicelli, but there's no need. It looks and tastes wonderful naked and unadorned.

Himself's Millionaire's Shortbread

Himself has no interest at all in sweet things. So all this cake stuff has been very boring for him. Nevertheless, he has been monumentally patient as I drone on beside him, chatting away to myself about caster sugar versus demerara sugar versus golden syrup. So there we were one day, me 'bouncing ideas off him' (i.e. forcing him to sit and endure while basically I intoned, 'Cake, cake, cake, cake, cake, cake, cake, cake,' over and over again) and somehow the conversation strayed on to Millionaire's Shortbread and how hard it would be to make. To my great surprise, he suddenly became very animated and stopped looking like a man considering setting himself on fire, sat up straight and said, 'No, it's really easy! I used to make it when I was a teenager!'

I can't tell you! It was like discovering he was secretly Argentinian and had enjoyed a moderately successful career as a polo player in his twenties. Intrigued, I pressed him further for details and this is what he gave me.

Makes 16

For the base
225g plain flour
80g caster sugar
175g butter, cut into cubes

For the caramel layer
400ml sweetened condensed milk*
200g butter
65ml golden syrup
  (or 4 tablespoons)

For the chocolate topping
150g milk chocolate
150g dark chocolate
  (70% cocoa solids)

*If it comes in a can of 397ml, that's grand. You needn't fret about the missing 3ml.

Butter a 20cm square tin and line the base with baking paper. Make sure the tin is at least 6cm deep. Preheat the oven to 160°C/325°F/gas 3.

Sieve the flour into a bowl. Add the sugar and butter. If you have a machine, blitz everything together until you have a sandy-looking mixture, but beware of overmixing – you don't want this to turn into a dough. If you don't have a machine, I'm afraid you'll have to rub in the butter by hand. Pile the mix into the prepared tin and prick the surface several times with a fork.

Bake for 30 to 40 minutes until it's no longer pale-looking. Don't let it overbake and become hard and crusty because you'll have trouble down the line when you come to cut it. Leave to cool on a wire rack.

Now for the caramel layer. Put the condensed milk, butter and golden syrup into a heavy-bottomed saucepan and heat gently. Then, stirring constantly, bring the temperature up until you reach bubbling point and keep it there for 5 to 8 minutes. Don't make the mistake that I did in the first few minutes of thinking that if the butter was melted, that we were bombs away. Himself came in, took one look at it and said, 'No, it's way too pale,' so I had to put the saucepan back on the heat for at least another 10 minutes. Don't be tempted to turn up the heat any further! The caramel must be made over a low heat to avoid it catching and burning. Eventually, the mixture will thicken and darken and change, so that when you allow the mixture to fall off the spoon, it makes light ribbons on the surface of the caramel.

Pour the caramel on top of the shortbread base and leave to cool for about an hour. For the chocolate topping, melt the chocolate (see page 20) and pour it over the caramelly layer. Leave to set, but not in the fridge, for at least a couple of hours.

Remove from the tin and carefully cut into sixteen cubes.

Christmas Cake without Fear
(aka Traditional Fruit Cake)

The very words 'Christmas Cake' bring memories of my childhood flooding back in an absolute avalanche. The Day the Christmas Cake Was Made was one of the biggest on the Keyes' calendar and *entre nous* – and perhaps unexpectedly – not always the most joyful.

It was usually done about a month before Christmas and my poor mother, the stress of it was terrible for her. The whole deal was TCMNF (The Cake Must Not Flop). And apparently anything – anything – could make the cake flop. Any loud noise. Any sudden movement. Any bad news. My memory is that we spent hours and hours and hours tiptoeing around the darkened house, conversing in whispers, the television and radio silenced. Under no circumstances must a shoe fall on the floor or a person burst into song (highly unlikely, given the tension). And if anyone opened the oven door, there was no telling, *simply no telling*, what awful consequences would ensue.

Another aspect that I vaguely remember – my stomach automatically clenching with cell-imprinted fear – was brown paper. The tin had to be wrapped in layer upon layer of brown paper, which extended far higher than the height of the tin. Like the silence, the brown paper was *of vital importance* to the success of the cake, and had to be secured with twine. (Love that word, twine. Far more interesting than mere string.) I could never get to the bottom of why the brown paper was needed – I've just rung my mother to ask her and she seemed to think it was something to do with preventing the cake from burning. (But she exhibited PTSD symptoms when I tried to get her to talk about it, so she's not the most reliable of witnesses. She told me that one year she was just so overwhelmed by the responsibility of Making the Christmas Cake that she gave up entirely and my brothers Niall and Tadhg came home from school to find her lying limp in an armchair, the cake half mixed and they – entirely clueless – had to take over. She says all she can remember from that terrible day is overhearing Tadhg saying, 'Feck in another egg.' Then a while later Niall saying, 'Feck in more flour.' She has no memory of how the cake eventually turned out because she says, 'None of you ever ate it anyway. It was all about the selection boxes with you lot, I don't know why I bothered.')

Anyway! On that cheerful note, I've decided to reclaim Christmas Cake. This is very similar to my mother's recipe, but without the fear.

One very important thing to note is that you need to begin this cake an entire week before you actually bake it, because that's how long the dried fruit needs to steep in the brandy. (To be quite honest, if you're stuck for time, steeping it overnight should do fine.) •••

Makes 14–16 slices

450g currants

200g sultanas

200g raisins

125g glacé cherries

75g chopped mixed peel

1 glass of brandy

275g butter, at room
   temperature

275g light brown soft sugar

5 eggs

350g plain flour

1 teaspoon ground mixed
   spice

1 teaspoon ground cinnamon

1 teaspoon ground ginger

½ teaspoon ground nutmeg

pinch of salt

75g ground almonds

grated zest of 1 lemon

Put the currants, sultanas, raisins, cherries and mixed peel into a bowl and pour in the glass of brandy. Cover the bowl with a cloth and leave to steep. Stir it daily so that, to quote my mother, 'Everything gets a chance.'

On the big day, begin by preparing your tin. Use a 20cm square tin or a 23cm round tin. Grease the base and sides of the tin with butter, then line the base and sides with two layers of baking paper, making sure that it reaches at least 6cm above the edge of the tin. Preheat the oven to 150°C/300°F/gas 2.

Cream the butter and sugar together until it's light, pale and fluffy. In a separate bowl or jug, beat the eggs and add them slowly to the butter/sugar mix, beating between each addition. If the mix curdles, add a tablespoon of flour and keep going. Sieve in the flour, spices and salt and fold through by hand. Finally, fold in the soaked fruit, the ground almonds and the lemon zest. My mother says, 'You need a strong right arm for this.' (Unless you're left-handed, of course.)

Transfer the mixture into the prepared tin, smooth the top out as best you can, then wrap the *outside* of the tin with yet another layer of baking paper – tied in place with twine, of course. Or string, if you can't get any twine. Finally, as best you can, because this is undeniably a tricky business, loosely drape a layer of baking paper over the top, so that the whole tin is encased in baking paper. This is to stop the top of the cake burning during the long baking process.

Bake for 4 hours, then do your Skewer Test (see page 23). The cake mightn't be done yet. Use your cop on and test regularly – perhaps every 15 minutes or so – until you're happy it's fully baked. Don't worry if it takes a long time. The cake just does take ages, it's a mammoth undertaking, it's as simple as that. Put the tin on a wire rack and wait until the cake is fully cold before you begin the lengthy unwrapping process. Serve it as it is and it should be delicious and very densely fruity.

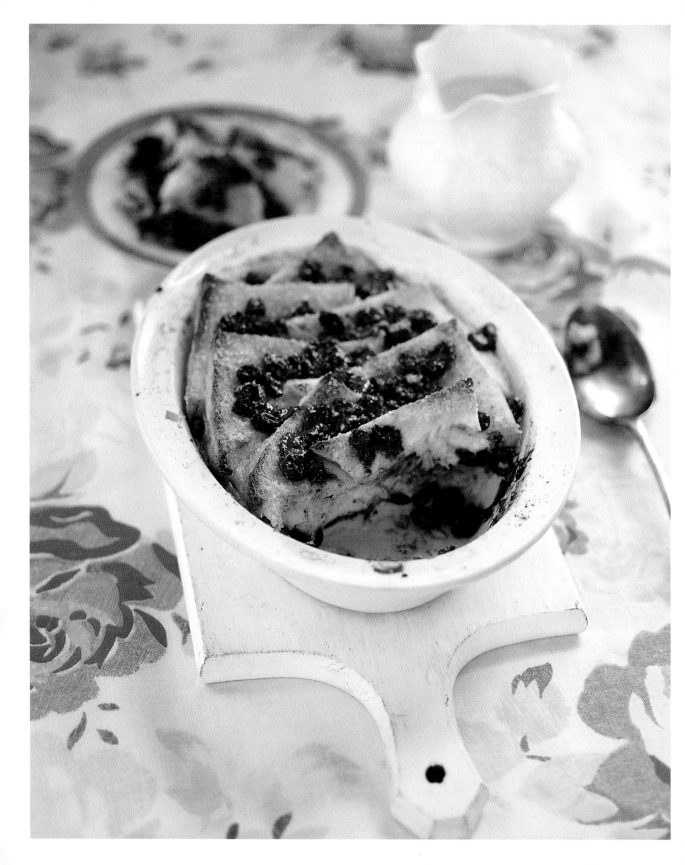

Bread and Butter Pudding

Bread and Butter Pudding is a 'housewife's favourite', they always say. A 'very economical way of using up stale bread'. Which sort of makes it sound like a bit of a joyless, half-hearted thing. But Bread and Butter Pudding is delicious, isn't it? I mean, it's FANTASTIC.

What I hadn't really taken on board is that the majority of Bread and Butter Pudding is custard. But Bread and Butter Pudding simply MUST be served *with* custard. Which could sound like custard overkill. But in my universe there is no such thing.

Finally, I have tried my very, very best to keep all the recipes in this section 'Classic'. However, here I've suggested adding some chocolate chips, which aren't classic, but please indulge me in this one small aberrance.

Serves 4–6

10 slices of white bread

50g butter, at room temperature

100g raisins

100g plain chocolate chips

¼ teaspoon freshly grated nutmeg

For the custard

300ml milk

100ml double cream

2 eggs

20g caster sugar

1 teaspoon vanilla extract

2 teaspoons demerara sugar

Very, very liberally, butter a 1 litre pie dish and preheat the oven to 180°C/350°F/gas 4. Cut the crusts off the slices of bread, butter them on one side, then cut them into triangles. Have them standing by with the raisins, chocolate chips and nutmeg. Because now, in an unexpected change of direction, we're going to make the custard.

In a saucepan, gently heat the milk and cream, but don't let them boil. In a separate bowl, beat the eggs with the caster sugar and vanilla extract until pale and fluffy. Slowly pour some of the warm milk into the egg mixture and beat well. Add more warm milk and continue beating until it's all added. Don't expect it to thicken because it won't. That's okay, it will 'set' while it's in the oven.

Now, back to the bread. Cover the base of the pie dish with one layer of bread triangles, butter side up. Overlap them slightly, making sure there are no gaps and that the dish 'floor' is fully covered. Sprinkle one third of the raisins and one third of the chocolate chips evenly over the bread, then lightly sprinkle with a little nutmeg. Then, very gently, pour a little of the custard over. Go very easy. Add just enough to cover the bread.

Now, lay down another layer of neatly overlapping bread triangles and sprinkle over another third of the raisins, chocolate chips and nutmeg. Pour over more of the custard mix.

Then lay down the third and final layer of bread triangles, raisins, chocolate chips and nutmeg. Now, carefully pour the remaining custard over the whole business, making sure that the liquid is evenly spread and that even the edges are soaked because they're the parts that are most likely to dry out during the baking process. Sprinkle the demerara sugar over the surface.

Bake for 40 to 45 minutes. The surface should be golden brown and the 'egginess' set.

CUPCAKES

Sweet and Simple Strawberry Cupcakes

B-list Chocolate-Chip Cupcakes

Consistently Reliable Cupcakes

Blondie Cupcakes

Carrot Cake Cupcakes

Slightly Sinister Star Anise Cupcakes

Zeny's Banoffee Cupcakes

Chocolate Cheesecake Cupcakes

Red Velvet Cupcake Swirls

Wasabi and White Chocolate Cupcakes
with Salted Caramel Icing

Okay, I know **CUPCAKES** have become a bit of a joke. I mean, we're overrun with the things. You can't go five yards without tripping over one. But they're ubiquitous for a reason: because they're lovely. They're an excellent little size. They're self-contained and unmessy in that you don't need a knife or a plate to eat them. And they can be decorated in the most adorable ways, which we'll get to.

For someone new to baking, cupcakes are brilliant because the ingredients are basic and the techniques are straightforward. The four basic requirements are flour, sugar, eggs and some sort of fat, usually butter. Flavouring is up to you: it can be as simple as a teaspoon of vanilla extract, or you can experiment with chocolate, dried fruit, nuts, citrus rinds, even tiny pieces of liquorice.

As for cupcake technique, have your butter and eggs at room temperature before you start. 'Cream' the butter and sugar, that is, beat them together with gusto until 'two-becomes-one' and they're fluffy and pale. What you're doing is incorporating air, which will help the end result be light and airy. Always beat your eggs before adding them to the mix and ALWAYS sieve your flour. I've even heard of people 'twice-sieving' their flour and sometimes even 'three-times-sieving' (that is, sieving it on to a plate, then putting it back in the sieve, sieving it on to the plate again, then finally sieving it into the mixing bowl, all in an attempt to incorporate more air). Even for those of us looking for any small job to get us through the day, this seems a little excessive.

Once the flour has been sifted in, it's time for a change of pace. No more gusto-stirring. Gently, now, all is gentle. What's happening is that we're 'folding' in the flour, that is, we're turning it into the mix with as little energy as possible. This is still all about the 'air' – we don't want to knock out the air we've gone to a lot of time and trouble to incorporate. Sometimes people suggest using a metal spoon for this exercise, but I prefer my purple spatula because it gets into all the nooks and crannies.

Using two tablespoons – one to scoop and the other to scrape off the scoopy one – dollop the mix (or 'batter' as some cake writers like to call it) into cupcake cases. The general rule is to fill the case two-thirds full to leave space for the much-heralded 'rising', but in some of the recipes here I've gone off piste with other suggestions.

Now, a word about cupcake cases. There is no standard size. When someone finally articulated this simple truth to me, it was as if I'd been let into the secret of the universe. I'd instinctively known that there was something I wasn't understanding when I was spooning cake mix into paper cases, but I didn't know what I didn't know, if you know what I mean. I now discover that there are different widths at the base, there are different widths at the top, there are different depths to the 'pleats' and there are different heights. All different. God knows how many variables we've got on our hands and there is no right or wrong, but it's important to know what you're dealing with. Personally I favour the taller, narrower paper case, but each to their own.

Bake at the suggested temperature for the suggested amount of time, but if you're not sure they're done, apply the Skewer Test (see page 23). Cool the tray on a wire rack for about 10 minutes, then – gently, because they're still very wobbly, like any newborn – take each cupcake, still in its paper case, out of the tray, but keep them cooling on the rack for about half an hour. You can now serve them as they are, or you can decorate with an icing (see page 51 for the basic Glacé and Buttercream icings), the choice is yours.

Buttercream Icing

Buttercream icing can be used in piping, or to give a cupcake 'height'.

Coats 12–16 cupcakes, depending on how generous you want to be

250g butter, at room
  temperature

350g icing sugar

1 teaspoon vanilla extract*

gel or liquid food colouring
  (optional)

*You can use a whole host
  of flavouring, it doesn't
  have to be vanilla

Slice the butter into chunks into a bowl. Slowly sieve in the icing sugar. Using an electric mixer on a very slow speed, beat the two together. (The reason for the slowness is – again – the pesky icing sugar.) If you're doing this in a KitchenAid, a handy tip is to throw a clean tea towel over the top of it to limit the distance the icing sugar travels out into the air.

When the icing sugar is incorporated, you can increase the speed until the icing is smooth and creamy. Add the vanilla extract and food colouring, if you're using, and beat again.

Basic Glacé Icing

Glacé icing is simple to make, and gives a flat finish.

Coats 12 cupcakes

300g icing sugar

2–3 tablespoons water
  or lemon or lime juice

gel food colouring**
  (optional)

**But it must be gel, not
  liquid, colouring because
  that will interfere with the
  runniness of the icing.

Slowly sieve the icing sugar into a big bowl – it needs to be done slowly because icing sugar puffs up into a big cloud and gets everywhere. (My entire house is coated in a thin film of it.)

Gradually add the water or juice and whisk until you get the runniness you'd like, always remembering that you can add more if you need to, but can't take any back out. However, if you feel it's gone too runny on you, simply add more icing sugar. Also, bear in mind that icing sugar is notoriously lumpy and the longer you beat it, the more lumps you will 'flush' out, so the thicker the icing will get. If you're using colouring gel, add it with a cocktail stick.

Use this icing immediately because it sets quickly. There are two ways (that I know of) to coat cupcakes with glacé icing:

You can 'dunk' the cupcake into the bowl of icing, surface side down. Give it a twirl so that the excess icing falls off, then turn the right way round.

OR

You can simply use a spoon to pour the icing on to the top of the cupcake and a knife to coax it evenly over the surface.

Sweet and Simple Strawberry Cupcakes

These are delicious little delights. Quick and easy to make, they come out super-light and airy and the fresh strawberries are a sweet surprise.

Makes 12

200g fresh strawberries
100ml sunflower oil
90g caster sugar
2 eggs
180g plain flour
¾ teaspoon bicarbonate
   of soda

Preheat the oven to 180°C/350°F/gas 4 and line a 12-hole cupcake tray with paper or silicone cases. Wash and hull the strawberries and mash until they're pulpy.

Beat the oil, sugar and eggs together for a few minutes until the mix starts to look caramelly. Add the pulped strawberries, sieve in the flour and bicarbonate of soda and fold through.

Pour the thinnish batter into the cases and bake for about 20 minutes. Cool on a wire rack and decorate pinkly.

B-List Chocolate Chip Cupcakes

The more fat a recipe has, the richer and more delicious it is. Because this recipe has only one egg, a smallish amount of butter and uses cocoa powder instead of melted chocolate, it's not the richest thing you'll ever taste, but you know what, it'll do grand. Like, it won't be disgusting or anything. It's quick and easy and good for serving to kids because they don't care about subtleties. Especially if you throw a few glittery sprinkles over the finished product. Or else you can balance the whole thing out by using a super-rich chocolate topping.

Makes 12

100g self-raising flour

20g cocoa powder
(70% cocoa solids)

140g caster sugar

50g butter

120 ml full-fat milk*

1 egg

½ teaspoon vanilla extract

100g milk chocolate chips
(optional)

For the (optional) topping

100g dark chocolate

55g butter, cut into cubes

255g icing sugar

65ml full-fat milk

½ teaspoon vanilla extract

*Must be full fat. Must be!

Preheat your oven to 170°C/325°F/gas 3 and line a 12-hole cup-cake tray with paper cases.

Mix the flour, cocoa powder, sugar and butter until the butter is absorbed and the whole business starts to look grainy. You can do this by hand, using an electric whisk or, if you're lucky enough to have a KitchenAid, using the paddle attachment.

In a separate bowl, whisk the milk, egg and vanilla extract together, then add to the flour mix, taking care not to overmix. Throw in the chocolate chips, if you're using them, and distribute evenly.

Divide the mix among the paper cases and bake for about 20 minutes, until the cupcake 'replies' when pressed. Or use your Skewer Test (see page 23). Cool on a rack.

Make the (optional) topping by melting the chocolate and butter in a saucepan over a very low heat, stirring constantly, until they've melted. Remove from the heat and gradually beat in the icing sugar, milk and vanilla, whisking until smooth. If you feel the icing is looking too runny to use straight away, refrigerate for 15 to 20 minutes.

A word of warning. Because of the low fat content, these cupcakes won't last long, even in an airtight tin.

Consistently Reliable Cupcakes

Very dependable little creatures, these. They always come out just right – just moist enough, just light enough, just rich enough. I've used vanilla here, but there's a huge choice of flavouring available and there are a few variations suggested at the end. I've recommended icing these cupcakes with buttercream and again suggested flavouring with vanilla, but once more, feel free to use whatever flavouring you like.

Makes 12

125g butter, at room
  temperature

125g caster sugar

2 eggs, beaten

1 vanilla pod*

125g self-raising flour

Buttercream icing

225g butter, at room
  temperature

300g icing sugar

1 teaspoon vanilla extract

gel or liquid food colouring
  (optional)

glitter or coloured sanding
  sugar (again optional, but
  why not go for it?)

*Or if that's a bit too exotic and scary, a teaspoon of vanilla extract. But preferably not vanilla essence, which is just a load of chemicals. Unless you're really stuck, and then work away. God knows, what harm can it do? I mean, they used to give babies gripe water, which is basically alcohol, and the human race has survived thus far.

Preheat your oven to 160°C/325°F/gas 3 if you'd like flat-topped cakes or 180°C/350°F/gas 4 if you'd like them roundy. Line a 12-hole cupcake tray with paper cases. IMPORTANT: ensure that you pick nice colours and patterns, ones that will make you happy.

Fling your butter into your bowl and cream the daylights out of it with an electric mixer, occasionally scraping the beaters with your purple spatula (see page 16). When you start to feel a little bored – perhaps after 5 minutes or so – add the sugar and keep beating until the whole mixture goes pale and fluffy.

Gradually add the eggs, beating well between each addition. Now brace yourself: the mix might curdle a bit, but DON'T PANIC. You've done nothing wrong, this is not your fault. It is an occasional and unpleasant fact of life, like for example a burst tyre, it happens to the best of us. Simply sieve in a little of the flour, keep beating valiantly and soon the problem will go away. If only everything in life was as fixable.

Next, the vanilla pod, not as daunting as it may sound. Slit it along its length and you will discover a load of seeds inside. Use a knife to scrape these out and fling them into the mix. Discard the rest.

Abandon the beaters, sieve in the flour and then gently 'fold' (i.e. incorporate) it into the mix, using as few turns of the spatula (or metal spoon) as possible. When you can't see any more flour lurking in the bowl, you're ready to go. Using two tablespoons, distribute the mix into the cupcake cases, filling them approximately two-thirds full.

Bake at 160°C for 22 minutes if you want flat-tops or 180°C for 18 to 20 minutes if you'd prefer dome-shaped. Or do the Skewer Test (see page 23). Cool on a wire rack and store in an airtight tin. They should keep for a day or so. Slightly longer if your tin has polka dots.

To make the icing, cut the butter into chunks into a bowl and slowly sieve in the icing sugar. On a very slow speed, beat the two together. When the icing sugar is incorporated, you can increase the speed until the icing is smooth and creamy. Add the vanilla extract and food colouring, if you're using, and beat again.

Use a mini palette knife to smooth the icing over the tops of the cupcakes. Or if you're feeling brave, use a piping bag with a star-shaped nozzle and pipe fat swirls. Finish with a sprinkle of glitter, coloured sanding sugar or whatever you're in the mood for.

Variations

By omitting the vanilla pod, you can use this same basic recipe to make a variety of flavours. For example, if you'd like orange flavouring, add the zest of half an orange. Or add a teaspoon of coffee dissolved in 2 tablespoons of boiling water for coffee flavour (cool it slightly before adding because it might scramble the eggs). Or sift a teaspoon of ground ginger in with the flour for ginger flavouring, and so on.

Blondie Cupcakes

Blondies are brownies made with white chocolate, which – you probably know this, if you're anything like the expert in chocolate that I am – has a milder, sweeter taste than milk or dark chocolate. Nevertheless, do not underestimate these cupcakes. They are not as innocuous as they might initially seem. They're full of flavour and the lovely crunch of the macadamia nuts really elevates them into something wonderful.

**Makes 12 generous cupcakes
or 16 medium ones**

100g butter
300g white chocolate
100g macadamia nuts*
3 eggs
100g soft brown sugar
1 teaspoon vanilla extract
180g plain flour
1 teaspoon baking powder
pinch of salt

*If you can get them
Hazelnuts if you can't.

Line one or two 12-hole cupcake trays with paper cases and preheat the oven to 170°C/325°F/gas 3.

In a heatproof bowl over a saucepan of hot water, gently melt the butter and 200g of the chocolate, remembering that white chocolate burns at the drop of a hat. Keep a good watch on it and stir often.

Roughly chop the remaining 100g white chocolate and the macadamia nuts and set aside. Whisk the eggs and sugar until thick and creamy. Add the vanilla extract and the melted chocolate/butter mix.

Sieve in the flour, baking powder and salt and fold through. Gently stir in the remaining chocolate and nuts.

Divide the mix among the paper cases and bake for about 20 minutes. Cool on a wire rack. Serve and watch the initially unimpressed faces of your guests transform into expressions of admiration and respect.

Carrot Cake Cupcakes

So good for the eyesight, carrots.

Makes 12

50g walnuts*

150g carrots

150g light muscovado sugar

2 medium eggs

150ml sunflower oil

150g plain flour

1 teaspoon bicarbonate of
soda

1 teaspoon baking powder

1 teaspoon ground ginger

1 teaspoon ground cinnamon

1 teaspoon ground nutmeg

For the icing

60g butter, at room
temperature

225g cream cheese

125g icing sugar

1 teaspoon vanilla extract

green food colouring**

To decorate (optional)

12 tablespoons Coco Pops

edible glitter, in green,
orange and bronze

approx. 30 marzipan
carrots***

*If you really must, I can't
stick them myself.

**I used Squires' Foliage
Green.

***Can be bought in cake
supply places or you
could try making your
own from marzipan and
orange food colouring.

Line a 12-hole cupcake tray with paper cases and preheat the oven to 170°C/325°F/gas 3. Roughly chop the walnuts – go on, really make them suffer, sour, bitter yokes that they are. (Sorry, forgive me, I just have a 'thing' about walnuts, even though other people swear by them.) Keep them standing by. Peel and finely grate the carrots and have them standing by too.

Beat the sugar, eggs and oil together until the mix looks like dark caramel. Sieve in the flour, bicarbonate of soda, baking powder, ginger, cinnamon and nutmeg and mix well. Add the chopped walnuts and grated carrots and stir until you feel everything is uniformly distributed.

Divide the mixture evenly among the paper cases. They'll come up quite high, but that's okay, they're too dense to do much rising. Bake for 18 to 25 minutes. Cool on a wire rack.

Now, it's perfectly acceptable to serve these cupcakes as they are. You don't have to do another single thing. But if you're in the mood to create something beautiful, you can decorate them in the manner I've suggested below.

Make the icing by beating the butter and cream cheese together. When they are well mixed, sieve in the icing sugar and beat slowly. When you feel it's all mixed, add the vanilla extract and beat again. Add the green food colouring until you get the colour you want. This is meant to represent grass, but I like everything to be larger than life. Using a mini palette knife, if you're lucky enough to own one, distribute the frosting over the top of each cupcake.

If you've decided you want to decorate further, scatter green glitter over half of the green icing. On the other half, scatter Coco Pops, taking care to press them into the icing so that they'll stay. Stick on the marzipan carrots, having most of them on the green 'grass', but with their narrowest bit 'growing' out of the 'earth' of the Coco Pops. Scatter some orange glitter over the carrots and bronze glitter over the Cocoa Pops. Serve and expect a fair bit of praise.

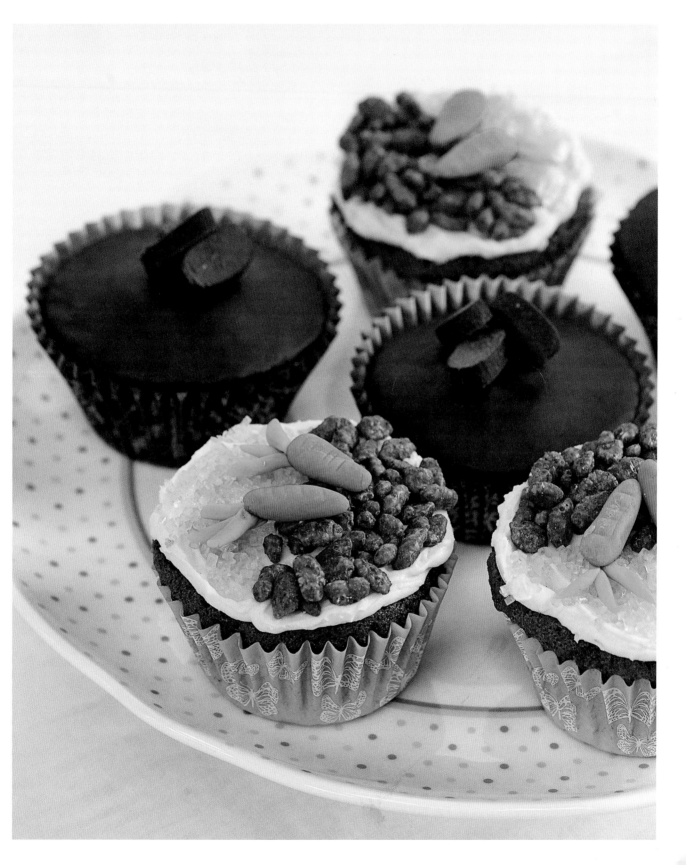

Slightly Sinister Star Anise Cupcakes

Star anise is some sort of spice, with a sweet liquorice, aniseedy flavour, which can be found in Asian food shops. I've also suggested adding actual pieces of liquorice (the soft, good-quality stuff you get in health food stores) to this recipe, but if it's too full on, reduce the amount or just leave it out altogether. Some people (particularly jazz lovers, I've found) are mad for these cupcakes, claiming that they're their absolute favourites, but others are a bit freaked out. Especially children. Sometimes they cry.

Just a quick note on sugar paste, in case you don't know what it is. It's a thick brick of icing that needs to be kneaded and softened, then rolled out. (You'll probably be most familiar with it from Christmas cakes.) Regular supermarkets sell it in white lumps, which you can colour into a multitude of gorgeous hues using gel from specialist bakeshops. To make black sugar paste, mix it with Squires' Extra Black colouring gel. Or Dr. Oetkers do a pack of five different colours of sugar paste, which includes black. Please don't be intimidated by sugar paste, it looks so fantastic on top of cakes.

Makes 12

4 stars of anise

200ml full-fat milk

115g butter

150g golden caster sugar

2 eggs

½ teaspoon vanilla extract

170g self-raising flour

½ teaspoon baking powder

pinch of salt

100g soft black liquorice, original flavour, chopped very, very, very finely

For the icing

150g black sugar paste

edible glue **OR** clear alcohol **OR** apricot jam that has been boiled and strained (to stick the sugar paste to the cupcakes).

5–6 pieces of soft black liquorice, chopped very finely

Bash the stars of anise with a mallet, hammer or any blunt instrument you might have handy. Pour the milk into a saucepan, then add the bashed star anise. 'Scald' the milk (see page 21), then leave for at least an hour for the liquorice flavour from the star anise to infuse into the milk.

When the hour is up, preheat the oven to 180°C/350°F/gas 4 and line a 12-hole cupcake tray with paper cases, preferably in a dark colour (black would be ideal).

Cream the butter and sugar, then add the eggs and vanilla extract. Sieve in the flour, baking powder and salt. Using a sieve, strain the milk into the mix, leaving the star anise behind. You can now discard these. Fold the mix carefully until all the flour is incorporated, then add the small pieces of chopped liquorice, distributing evenly.

Divide the mix among the cupcake cases, bake for approximately 20 minutes, then cool on a wire rack.

You can serve them undecorated, but if you'd like to decorate them, lightly dust your surface with icing sugar and roll out the sugar paste. Using one of your shamefully large collection of cookie cutters (if you're me), cut out twelve circles, each slightly wider than the surface of the cupcakes. Stick the circles of sugar paste on to the cupcakes using edible glue, clear alcohol or apricot jam. Attach the pieces of liquorice to the top of the cupcakes (see a photo of the cakes on page 61). Eat, wearing a black polo neck jumper and listening to mid-period Miles Davis.

Zeny's Banoffee Cupcakes

These aren't mere cupcakes, these are *events:* banana sponge with a heart of dulce de leche and luscious toffee-flavoured cream cheese frosting.

I'd bought a big bunch of bananas in the vague hope that the potassium might help, but then I hadn't the energy to peel them. They were sitting on the worktop, getting more and more ripe while I was feeling more and more guilty, and then my lovely friend Beth was over and, without prompting, wrote out her sister Zeny's foolproof banana bread recipe and suddenly I was reinvigorated.

I've adapted the recipe slightly to make it more suitable for cupcakes and I've added toffee to make the 'offee' bit, but obviously you can leave it out and still have monumentally delicious banana cupcakes.

First, a word about dulce de leche. It's an Argentinian dessert, which literally translates as 'sweet milk'. (Mind you, the one time I was in Argentina I actually had it for my breakfast, but that's the type I am.) It's a delicious, gooey, toffee-caramel style thing with a texture like thick set custard. You could make it yourself, but it's a fiendishly tedious exercise because it involves hanging around a saucepan of simmering milk for the best part of a day. Also, I believe it can be produced by boiling a can of condensed milk for 4 hours (I saw it done by Emile Heskey's girlfriend on *Celebrity Come Dine with Me*), but then I read a horror story on the internet about someone's saucepan boiling dry and the tin of condensed milk exploding. So I buy my dulce de leche ready made. Obviously, there's a variety of authenticity and quality available – there's some very high-class stuff, which is handmade by tango-dancing gauchos wearing shoes that used to belong to Eva Perón's next-door-neighbour. Or you can buy it mass-produced in a can, which makes me feel a bit Jeremy Kyle, but it's actually delicious. ● ● ●

Makes 12

125g butter

125g caster sugar

2 eggs, beaten

3 or 4 very ripe bananas

125g self-raising flour

approx. 500g dulce de leche
(You'll only need about 80g
for the cakes, but you can
use the rest for icing.)

For the icing

50g butter

90g cream cheese

180g icing sugar

Preheat the oven to 170°C/325°F/gas 3 and line a 12-hole cupcake tray with paper cases.

Cream the butter and sugar until pale and fluffy, then add the beaten eggs. Mash the bananas and gently add to the mix, then sieve in the flour and fold until it's all absorbed.

Now, this is where the challenge begins. Using two tablespoons, and at times maybe even your fingers, distribute about two-thirds of the cake mix into the paper cases, making sure the entire base of each case is covered. Then – and this is the fiddliest bit – gently place a small round dollop, about the size of a Malteser, of dulce de leche into the middle of each cupcake. (I use a melon baller to do this, it gives a very handy shape and size.)

Next – again using your fingers if you have to, this is delicate work – distribute the remaining cake mix into the paper cases, completely covering the dulce de leche and making sure that the edges of the 'bottom' layer of cake mix are adhering to the top. The idea is that you're making a little dulce de leche bomb. On the outside it looks just like an ordinary cupcake. But then a person bites into it and – oho! A delightful caramelly surprise is awaiting within.

I'll be honest, getting these right can be tricky because you don't want the dulce de leche sinking to the bottom and just sort of leaking away. It's about having the base layer thick enough to withstand the weight, while still having enough cake mix left over to put a lid on things and seal the whole little envelope.

Practice is the key. Practice and patience. Practice, patience and perseverance. Practice, patience, perseverance and persistence. (Can I think of anything else beginning with P? 'Praise', how about that? Praise the cakes for holding up the dulce de leche. It's all about positive affirmation. If you tell them they can support the dulce de leche, then they'll believe they can.)

Bake for at least 25 minutes, maybe even half an hour. I know it sounds like a long time, but it's because of the bananas.

Now, for the icing. You can keep things simple and simply put a layer of dulce de leche on the top of each little cake. Or you can make things slightly more complicated by diluting the dulce de leche with cream cheese frosting.

Mix 400g of the dulce de leche with the butter, cream cheese and icing sugar until it's thick and creamy, then smooth it over the cupcakes. Or, if you're feeling like more of a challenge, pile it all into a piping bag with a star-shaped nozzle and squeeze it out in big, fat, fabulous swirls.

Chocolate Cheesecake Cupcakes

Try saying that with loose dentures. These are very special – they're not really cupcakes at all, they're mini cheesecakes, but in cupcake format (albeit without the biscuit base) – and they are *delicious*.

Makes 12

100g dark chocolate
(70% cocoa solids)

250g mascarpone cheese

200g Philadelphia full-fat
cheese*

100g caster sugar

2 eggs

1 teaspoon vanilla extract

100g milk chocolate chips

*Not the low-fat version.
Or the one with garlic
and herbs.

Line a 12-hole cupcake tray with paper cases and preheat the oven to 150°C/300°F/gas 2.

Melt the chocolate using your preferred method (see page 20). Beat the cheeses, then add the sugar, eggs and vanilla extract and beat again. Using your purple spatula (see page 16), add the melted chocolate and mix well, then throw in your chocolate chips, doing your best to distribute them evenly, but not going all OCD about it.

Divide the mix among the paper cases. Fill generously. You might have a moment of panic when you think you have too much mixture, but the thing is that these cupcakes don't really rise, so it's okay to fill the cases almost to the top.

Now we're going to do something that sounds trickier than it actually is: we're going to 'bain-marie' these boyos. Basically, you put your metal cupcake tray into a bigger, deeper tin (like a roasting tin, for example). Pour warm – not boiling – water into the bigger, deeper tin so that it comes about three-quarters of the way up the side of the cupcake tray, then place – with great caution – in the oven.

Bake for 40 minutes then – again, with great caution, in fact with much *greater* caution because by now the water is scalding hot   take it all out. Pour away the water and place the cupcake tray on a cooling rack. Leave it about an hour before you take the cupcakes out of the tin because they have to sort of 'set'. But you can't eat them just yet, they need to be refrigerated. Could you bear to do it overnight?

Serve with a dollop of whipped cream and, can I just say something, these cupcakes may not look like anything special, but when a person takes a bite, they sort of freeze, then they yelp, 'Oh my good Christ, what just happened there?' And the next thing they're tearing at the cupcake with their nails, shovelling it into their mouths and lunging at you and demanding more.

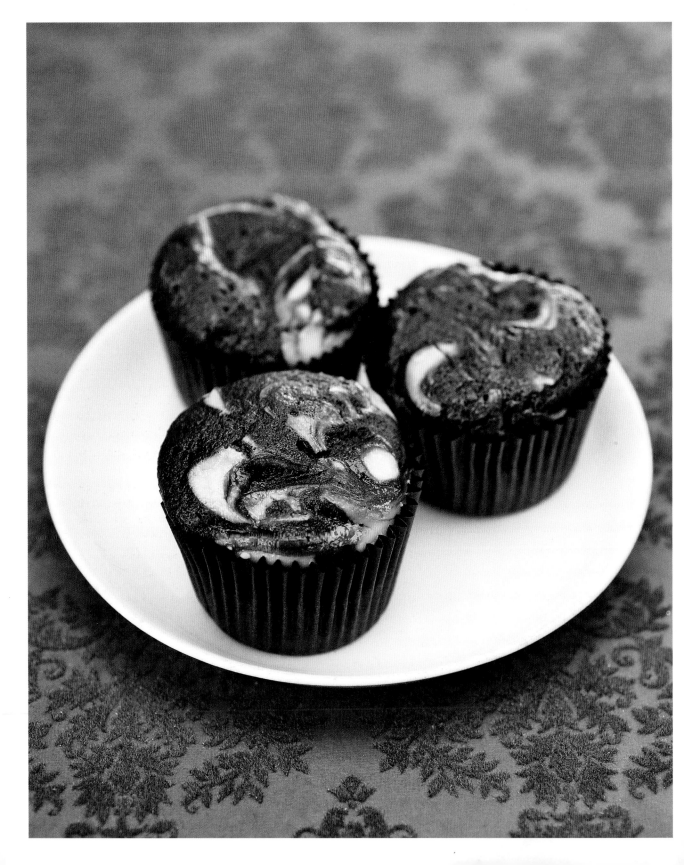

Red Velvet Cupcake Swirls

According to my research, Red Velvets date from the olden days when cocoa powder was a much lighter colour than it is now. During the baking process, the acid in the cake mix (sometimes provided by buttermilk, sometimes, as in this recipe, by vinegar) chemically reacted to create the distinctive red colour. Nowadays though, with cocoa powder being so dark, the red colour is provided by food colouring. Nevertheless, the yumminess remains the same.

It seems to be a given that Red Velvets are served with cream cheese frosting, but I've gone a little experimental here and incorporated a cream cheese layer into the mix, so the frosting is 'built in', if you get me. It is 'swirled through' and actually baked into each little cake, which not only looks beautiful, but means you don't have to do any decorating or icing at the end.

Makes 12

For the red velvet layer

110g butter

170g caster sugar

1 teaspoon vanilla extract

40g cocoa powder

a pinch of salt

1 tablespoon red food colouring*

1 teaspoon white wine vinegar

2 eggs

160g self-raising flour

For the cream cheese layer

200g cream cheese

1 egg

40g caster sugar

½ teaspoon vanilla extract

*I used Squires' Extra Red Gel.

Line a 12-hole cupcake tray with paper cases and preheat the oven to 170°C/325°F/gas 3.

First, make the cream cheese layer by beating the cream cheese with the egg, sugar and vanilla extract. Keep it standing by.

Make the red velvet mix by melting the butter. Put into a bowl with the sugar and beat well. Next – in this exact order! Something to do with chemical jiggery-pokery that I can't explain, but must be observed – add the vanilla extract, the cocoa powder, the salt, the food colouring and the vinegar, beating between each addition.

In a separate bowl, beat your eggs, then add to the butter/cocoa mix. Sieve in the flour and fold through.

Divide most of the mix among the paper cases, reserving perhaps a fifth. Then, dollop a lump of cream cheese mix into each paper case on top of the red velvet mix. *Then*, divide the remaining red velvet mix into the paper cases, on top of the cream cheese mix.

Now, *swirl*. You can use a cocktail stick, but I used a bamboo skewer – something with a bit of length is nice because you can get right down into the red velvet mix and dredge up its murky depths – and twirl and swirl until the red and white mixes are beautifully striped. This is an *extremely* enjoyable exercise, so enjoyable that I never want to stop, but I must because if I don't, the two mixes will become one and the whole thing will be pointless.

Bake for 17 to 20 minutes. Cool fully on a wire rack.

Wasabi and White Chocolate Cupcakes with Salted Caramel Icing

Yes, I'm serious. Wasabi. The stuff you have with sushi. But trust me, this isn't a game of novelty cupcakes, this recipe is *gorgeous*. The sweetness of the white chocolate combined with the richness of the eggs is powerful enough to go head-to-head with the heat of the wasabi. Then, paired with the salted caramel icing, the whole experience becomes transcendent.

If you really remain unconvinced by the wasabi, just leave it out. It's a great cupcake recipe anyway – it gives a very moist, rich crumb. And the salted caramel icing is *amazing*. Make sure you use it in lots of recipes – on brownies, as a topping for ice cream, whatever you can think of.

Makes 12

For the cupcakes
100g white chocolate
100g butter, chilled and cut into cubes
110g caster sugar
1 teaspoon vanilla extract
3 eggs
75g plain flour
1 teaspoon baking powder
pinch of salt
1 tablespoon wasabi paste

For the salted caramel topping
100g butter
75g light brown soft sugar
75g golden syrup
1 teaspoon vanilla extract
1 teaspoon coarse sea salt

Line a 12-hole cupcake tray with paper cases and preheat the oven to 180°C/350°F/gas 4.

Melt the chocolate using your favoured method (see page 20), remembering that this is white chocolate and is easy to burn. Add the butter to the chocolate and stir until everything is melted and combined. Remove from the heat and stir in the sugar. The mix might look a little strange and 'congealy'. Don't worry. Let it all cool for about 10 minutes, then add the vanilla extract and beat with an electric mixer for a full 3 minutes. This should sort out any nonsense. Add an egg and beat for at least 30 seconds. Add the next egg, and so on, until all are in. Sieve in the flour, baking powder and salt and fold through. Finally – if you're going to be brave – add a tablespoon of wasabi paste and make sure it's distributed evenly. Divide the mixture among the cupcake cases. Bake for 22 minutes. Cool the tray on a wire rack.

Meanwhile, make the salted caramel topping by putting the butter, brown sugar, golden syrup, vanilla and salt into a heavy-bottomed saucepan and melt over a gentle heat. When the butter and sugar have melted, raise the heat. Whisk like mad until the mix starts bubbling, but don't let it boil. Keep it at that bubbling point for about 5 to 8 minutes and it should thicken a little. But beware! This thing is horrifyingly hot and impossible to get off if you get splashed with it. Treat it with caution.

When you're satisfied with its consistency, let it cool a little before icing the cupcakes – if it's too hot, it's liable to run down the sides. However, if it cools down too much, it won't spread easily enough. So feel free to reheat it a bit if it's got too stubborn and resistant, or let it cool down if it's gone a little free-spirited with itself. Finish by sprinkling the top with a few grains of sea salt.

CHEESECAKES

'Black Hole' Chocolate Cheesecake

Individual Amaretto Cheesecakes

Blokey Snickers Cheesecake Loaf

Lavender and White Chocolate Cheesecake

No-Bake Ginger and Lime Cheesecake

Rosewater and Coconut Cheesecake

Fridge-Set Honeycomb Cheesecake

Upside-Down Saffron, Mint and Pomegranate Cheesecake

There are two kinds of cheesecakes – the baked kind and the non-baked kind – and they're both GORGEOUS. **CHEESECAKES** are very much about the texture: the baked ones should be dense enough to get me to emit an involuntary low moan of pleasure and the non-baked should be smooth and creamy, but, either way, cheesecake is not the sort of thing to make if you're looking for INSTANT GRATIFICATION. If a sugar craving comes at you, find some other way of addressing it because the unvarnished truth is that some relationships last longer than the time it takes to make cheesecake.

It's not that there's huge amounts of work involved in baking cheesecakes, but there are long periods of waiting, while some sort of magic happens, and I know of no way of speeding these up. But the wait is worth it, I promise you.

First, the base. Almost all of the recipes here involve melted butter mixed with some sort of crushed biscuit – I've varied the biscuits quite a bit because I started to become a little weary of digestives after a while. In some cases, I've recommended that the base be baked briefly, but all of them need to be refrigerated and ideally it should be overnight (or if you're really desperate, stick it in the freezer for 20 minutes).

The reason for this is to 'set' the base to allow it to retain its own identity, if you know what I mean, so that the cheesecake itself doesn't just overrun and swamp it. Firm delineation between the two is important: your mouth needs to know what's going on. 'Yes, I see,' it should be able to think, 'I'm currently eating the baked cheesecake part and I'm going to emit an involuntary low moan of pleasure and now, I'm eating something different. I'm eating the crunchy biscuit base and my, how agreeable the contrast between the two textures is.'

No-bake cheesecake usually sets in 3 hours, which might sound long, but it's nothing in comparison with the baked version, which is a right marathon. But as I keep saying, it's worth it. There is something about baked cheesecake that benefits from the ageing process, like fine wine and George Clooney.

The mixing of the cheesecake itself is a simple enough business – all involving some combination of cream cheese, eggs, sugar, cream and flavouring. And even the baking times aren't that long, between 40 minutes and an hour and a half. But when the baking time is up, I recommend that, without opening the oven door, you turn the heat off and let the cake stay in there, for at least an hour and possibly even overnight.

And even then it isn't ready to be eaten – it needs to be refrigerated. I'm so sorry! Could you bear to do it for 6 hours? Or even longer? I'm not just being cruel, something beyond our ken is happening inside the cheesecake. Strange forces are at work and at a molecular level it's changing and deliciousness is developing at an exponential rate.

Finally – and it might be 48 hours after you first started making it – your cheesecake will be ready to eat and I promise you, oh I promise you, you'll be glad you waited.

A couple of other points. In some recipes I've suggested using Philadelphia cheese, but you must use the full-fat version. You see, any so-called 'low-fat' cheese has been diluted with air and water and you might be able to fool yourself that it's delicious on your slice of toast, but it'll ruin your cake. Also, try not to do what I did one unhappy evening and accidentally buy the Garlic and Herbs version.

Finally, see the Techniques and Helpful Hints section (page 22) for how to get your cheesecake out of the tin.

'Black Hole' Chocolate Cheesecake

So called because it's so dense it seems to collapse under the weight of its own fabulousness. Eating a slice of this is like being punched in the stomach with a chocolate-flavoured fist. Stupendous.

Serves 10

For the base

100g dark chocolate
 (70% cocoa solids)
50g butter
200g digestive biscuits

For the filling

200g dark chocolate
 (70% cocoa solids)
200g mascarpone cheese
200g Philadelphia cheese –
 the full-fat variety*
50g golden caster sugar
2 eggs
1 teaspoon vanilla essence
¼ teaspoon black pepper**
150ml double cream

*Remember what I said, you're only ruining it for yourself otherwise.

**I know, strange, but trust me.

Grease the sides and line the base of a 23cm springform tin with baking paper.

To make the base, melt the chocolate using your favoured method (see page 20), then melt the butter in a saucepan.

Break the biscuits roughly, using the method on page 22.

When the biscuits are completely annihilated, mix them with the melted butter and chocolate, then press them into the springform tin, completely coating the base and bringing a little 'lip' up the sides. To make the surface smooth and even, I've found – oddly – that pressing a potato masher against it does the job. Stick in the fridge for at least an hour.

To make the filling, preheat the oven to 170°C/325°F/gas 3. Melt the chocolate and let it cool a little.

With much gusto, whip the cheeses with the sugar, eggs, vanilla and black pepper. Really give this your best shot so all the lumps are gone. This is one situation where an electric whisk is a godsend. The first cake I ever made was this one – I did it all by hand and my arm nearly had to be hospitalized.

Pour in the cream and keep whisking. Finally add the cooling chocolate and – yes – keep whisking. When it's all mixed and there are no white bits left to be seen, pour the mix in on top of the set biscuit base and bake for 40 minutes. Then, without opening the door, turn off the oven and let the cake sit in there for at least 2 hours, preferably overnight.

During the cooking time, your cake will have risen, but it will slowly sink back into itself. This isn't a bad thing. Not at all. It is simply becoming the cheesecake version of a black hole, the densest, most chocolatey thing in the universe. When you finally remove it from the oven, you'll stagger under the weight and Professor Brian Cox might show up to do a programme about it.

But it's not time to eat it yet. No, I'm sorry! Into the fridge with it, for at least 6 hours, preferably overnight. It's harsh to deprive you, but this cake really benefits from the wait.

Finally, spring the catch on the tin and release the cake into the wild.

Individual Amaretto Cheesecakes

This recipe gives you 6 mini-cheesecakes, each one more than enough for one person. These are elegant, grown-up cheesecakes – the base comes courtesy of crushed amaretti biscuits and the flavour of the filling is provided by amaretto liqueur. (The alcohol does evaporate during the cooking process, but if you'd prefer to steer clear, just use a teaspoon of almond essence instead.)

Makes 6

For the base
150g amaretti biscuits
40g butter

For the filling
360g Philadelphia cheese
80g caster sugar
2 small eggs, separated
3 tablespoons amaretto
  liqueur

Preheat the oven to 150°C/300°F/gas 2.

I suggest making these in a 6-hole muffin tin (the holes being 8cm in diameter). Grease liberally. I'm lucky enough to own a silicone muffin 'tin' so I don't have to grease anything, which I'm grateful for because even though it doesn't take long, I find it a tedious business. If you can't face the greasing process and you don't have a silicone tin, you could even use muffin cases.

Melt the butter and crush the amaretti biscuits (see page 22 for biscuit crushing suggestions). Mix the two together, then press down hard into the tin, using the base of a glass.

Bake for 15 minutes, take out of the oven, cool down, then refrigerate for at least an hour.

To make the filling, preheat the oven again to 150°C/300°F/gas 2.

In one bowl, beat the cheese, sugar and egg yolks. Add the amaretto or almond essence, whichever you're using.

In a separate bowl, beat the egg whites until soft peaks form. Gently fold this into the cheese mix.

Still being gentle – you want to keep as much air as possible in this – spoon it on top of the amaretti biscuit base.

Bake for 40 minutes. If you happen to glance through the oven window, you'll see that they'll puff up and rise alarmingly high, but don't worry, they'll calm down again.

When the 40 minutes is up, don't open the door, but turn off the oven, and leave the cakes sitting there for a couple of hours.

Then – yes, you've heard this before – refrigerate overnight.

Blokey Snickers Cheesecake Loaf

Snickers is an essentially blokey thing, no? I've always thought it's the sort of sweetmeat that men take a big chomp out of just before they abseil down the side of a mountain and, for a while, I thought it was the law that Snickers could only be eaten by men speeding past me on mountain bikes. Inspired by such rugged outdoorsiness, this is a hefty, hearty cheesecake, specially for the boys. The loaf format is an extra little touch on my part; I think it makes it even more manly.

Makes 10 substantial slices

For the base

150g milk chocolate
  digestive biscuits

50g salted peanuts

75g butter

For the filling

250g mascarpone cheese

250g ricotta cheese

100g caster sugar

2 eggs

200ml sour cream

4 Snickers bars, chopped into
  chunks

To decorate

squeezy toffee sauce out of a
  squeezy bottle

a generous handful of salted
  peanuts

Preheat the oven to 170°C/325°F/gas 3.

Line a 1kg loaf tin with baking paper – see the technique on page 20.

In a food processor, whizz the biscuits and peanuts so they form a rough-cut, rustic-looking mix; you should still be able to see parts of the peanuts. The first time I did it, I left the machine running so long that I accidentally made peanut butter and the whole thing went into a brown paste. Although I soldiered on, the base never really set, and I ended up having to do it all again. But that's okay, I make the mistakes so you don't have to.

Melt the butter and stir it through the crumbs. Even when you think it's fully mixed, give it a few more stirs. Pour the biscuit/peanut/butter mix into the bottom of the loaf tin and pack down hard, using the base of a glass. Bake for 15 minutes, remove from the oven and cool, then refrigerate, preferably overnight.

To make the filling, preheat the oven again to 170°C/325°F/gas 3. Mix the two cheeses together, then add the sugar and eggs. Pour in the sour cream, then stir in the Snickers pieces. Pour in on top of the biscuit base.

Bake for an hour and a half, then turn off the oven and leave it sitting there for as long as you can bear. When you eventually take it out, you'll be delighted to see the top has developed a gorgeous fudgey look. Refrigerate overnight.

To get the cake out of the tin, you'll need your palette knife. Slide it gently between the baking paper and the side of the tin, loosening all the way along. Then – do your best here, but don't wreck your head – try to bend the palette knife slightly to get it actually under the base of the cake. When you feel you can't get any further without breaking the cake or starting to cry, call a halt, then use the overhanging edges of the baking paper as 'handles' to lift the entire cake out of the tin. You might have to to-and-fro a little, as in, lift it a bit, then use the palette knife to do a bit more loosening, then lift it a bit more, until it's fully ready to emerge. Peel the paper off, then drizzle the toffee sauce and scatter the peanuts over the top. Cut into thick slices and serve to blokes.

Lavender and White Chocolate Cheesecake

I know what you're thinking. You're thinking *lavender*? You're thinking why would I want to eat a cheesecake that tastes like an aromatherapist's couch?

Fair enough, I know it's an oddish one, but will you give it a go? Will you go on this journey with me? I mean, what's the worst that can happen? Even if you hate it, we've still lived a little, taken a risk, essayed a small step into the unknown.

Makes 10 slices

For the base
75g butter
150g rich tea biscuits

For the filling
Lavender flavouring
  (see method)
200g white chocolate
200g mascarpone cheese
200g ricotta cheese
200g Philadelphia full-
  fat cheese
2 eggs
50ml double cream
claret/grape and pink food
  colouring gel (optional,
  but a nice touch)
edible purple glitter
  (again optional, but
  again a nice touch)

Right, first the lavender flavouring. Well, there's actually a few ways we can address it.

1. Use dried lavender. There are a few companies on the internet that do it and you can add it directly into your mix – 3 tablespoons gives a subtle but nice flavour. The thing about this method is that you get 'bits' in your mix, which some people think look rustic and authentic and which other people think look a bit alarming. It's a personal thing.

2. Infusion. Put 3 tablespoons of dried edible lavender into a saucepan with the 50ml double cream. Heat gently – don't let it get anywhere near boiling – then put aside for at least an hour.

3. You can actually get liquid lavender flavouring that is edible (i.e. not an essential oil. Please don't use essential oil. I'm not sure exactly what will happen to you if you do, but it mightn't be good). Unfortunately, the liquid flavouring is a rare and elusive beast – I found mine by complete accident in a funny shop in rural France – but you might be able to get it on the internet. The brand is Déco Relief (I know! How peculiar!) and the packaging describes itself as '*Arôme Naturel Concentré*', and they're not joking about the '*Concentré*' bit. Taken neat it's absolutely disgusting, so a little goes a very long way. The trick is to introduce it gradually – I added it literally a half a teaspoon at a time, tasting after each go. In the end I used 3 teaspoons and I nearly overdid it, but managed to rein myself back just in time. • • •

Choose your method and now let's begin. Line the base of a 23cm springform tin and grease the sides. Make the base by melting the butter and crushing the biscuits in a food processor or with a mallet in a plastic bag (see page 22). Mix the two thoroughly, pile it all into the tin and press down hard with the back of a spoon until it's tightly packed and smooth. Refrigerate for at least an hour.

To make the filling, heat the oven to 150°C/300°F/gas 2.

Melt the chocolate. As we know, white chocolate 'suffers with its nerves'. It's even more prone to burning than dark or milk chocolate, so take extra care with it. Whatever melting method you use (see page 20) do it slowly. Keep stirring. Keep watching and err on the side of caution. Take it off the heat before it's fully melted because the heat will keep working. When you're happy that it's done, let it cool slightly.

Cream the three cheeses together, getting all the lumps out. Add the melted chocolate and beat again. Then add in the eggs.

Now for the lavender. If you've decided to use the dried edible flowers, simply fire in 3 tablespoons, add the double cream and proceed to colouring.

If you're using the infusing method, strain the double cream through a sieve, leaving the lavender pieces behind (they can now be discarded). Add the cream to the mix and proceed to colouring.

Or if you've managed to track down the '*Arôme Naturel Concentré*', start adding it very gradually. Keep tasting and the minute you start to notice it, stop! Then add the double cream and proceed to colouring.

Colouring. Using a cocktail stick, add a tiny amount of claret/grape gel and mix well. Keep adding and stirring until it starts to look lovely and lavendery. To my alarm, the colour started to veer in the direction of grey, so I added a little dab of pink to cheer it. That made it too pink, so I added some more claret/grape and the final colour was a bit too dark to qualify as lavender, but I still thought it was beautiful.

When you're happy with the look, pour the mix on top of the chilled biscuit base and bake. Thirty minutes into the cooking time, open the oven and cover the cake loosely with a sheet of tinfoil – this is to keep the top from browning even slightly. You've gone to a lot of time and trouble to get that lavender colour and you don't want it corrupted.

Cook for a further 10 minutes, then turn off the oven but let the cake sit in there for at least an hour. Refrigerate overnight, sprinkle with purple glitter, then ... and this is a radical suggestion, but would you consider giving this cake away?

I just feel that this is a cake for giving to others. It looks so pretty and tastes so delicate and delicious. Anyone you give it to will be touched and delighted and you in turn will feel touched and delighted.

No-Bake Ginger and Lime Cheesecake

This is lovely. The spicy heat of the ginger biscuits works really well with the sharp tang of the lime. And the texture is different to that of baked cheesecake – this is very light and creamy. Because there's no actual baking involved, this cheesecake is ready a lot quicker than the previous cheesecake recipes I've given.

All the same, it's not what you might call speedy. There's still a lot of sitting around in fridges being done.

Serves 8

For the base
150g ginger nut biscuits
50g butter

For the topping
2 x 135g packets of lime jelly
200ml evaporated milk
200g cream cheese*
zest and juice of 3 limes
edible green glitter
 (optional, but I'd really
 recommend it)
whipped cream for
 decorating (optional)

*Any kind you like, even yes, if you like, on this one occasion, low fat. (Because there's no cooking involved, it won't flop on you.)

Crush the biscuits to a fine powder in a food processor or with a mallet in a plastic bag (see page 22). Melt the butter and add, mixing thoroughly, then press hard into the bottom of a 20cm springform tin. Put in the fridge for at least an hour.

Dissolve one of the packets of lime jelly by cutting the jelly into cubes, putting them into a heatproof jug or bowl, adding 100ml boiling water and stirring briskly. The instructions on the packet might say to use more water, but don't. If 100ml water doesn't fully dissolve the jelly, don't add more water. Instead, put the container of water and jelly into the microwave for a minute or so. Leave to cool fully.

Whisk the evaporated milk until it's light and foamy. Add in the cream cheese and beat very well until all the lumps are gone and the mix is smooth. Add the cooled jelly, the zest of 2 limes and the juice of 3 (hold on to the remaining zest for decorating purposes).

Pour this creamy mix on top of the ginger biscuit base, spread smoothly with your spatula, then put it back in the fridge for 3 hours.

When the 3 hours are up, make the second packet of lime jelly by dissolving it in 100ml boiling water. Allow it to cool completely, then stir in a teaspoon of edible green glitter. Carefully pour this over the top of the cheesecake so it covers it all, sitting in a thin layer. Back into the fridge with it for at least another hour.

Decorate with splodges of whipped cream and the remaining lime zest.

Rosewater and Coconut Cheesecake

Again, with the funny flavours, I hear you cry. First the lavender, now the rosewater. But the rosewater isn't really that unusual – isn't it used in Turkish delight? And the coconut is quite subtle.

Serves 10

For the base

I've actually got two options for you:

Option 1

260g Turkish delight biscuits

100g butter

OR

Option 2

150g packet of pink wafer vanilla-sandwich biscuits

50g butter

For the filling

200g mascarpone cheese

300g Philadelphia cheese

200ml full-fat coconut milk (from a tin)

2 eggs

70g desiccated coconut

2 capfuls of rosewater

pea-sized ball of pink food colouring gel

As I write, Turkish delight biscuits are just new on the shelves in Ireland and they're so exciting and DELICIOUS. They're milk-chocolate covered biscuits with, I quote from the packaging, 'Turkish delight flavoured jam'. I suspect they're a bit of a novelty item and won't have the staying power of, say, your HobNobs or your ginger nuts. They probably won't be around for long, so if you can't get them, don't worry. Use the pink wafer version or a basic digestive biscuit mix (150g of biscuits and 50g of melted butter).

However, if you can get them, take a moment to feel blessed, then use a food processor to grind them to fine crumbs – I wasn't able to achieve this with the mallet alone, I think it must be the jam that complicated things.

Line the base of a 23cm springform tin and grease the sides. Melt the butter and add to the biscuits, mixing well, then pack into the tin and refrigerate for an hour or more.

Or, if you're using the pink wafer biscuit option, crush them in a food processor or with a mallet in a plastic bag (see page 22). Melt the butter and mix in, then pack into the tin and refrigerate for 15 minutes. This gives a thin, crisp, very sweet – some might say *too* sweet – base.

To make the filling, preheat the oven to 170°C/325°F/gas 3. Beat the cheeses, coconut milk and eggs. Stir in the desiccated coconut, rosewater and pink food colouring, if you're using it. Just for the record, I added some pink glitter to the unbaked mix, but it just disappeared – there was nothing at all shiny about the finished cake.

Pour the mix on top of the base and bake for 45 minutes. For the last 15 minutes, cover loosely with a sheet of tinfoil. This is to stop the top browning and doing away with your lovely pink colour.

Turn off the heat, then leave the cake in the oven for at least an hour. Refrigerate overnight.

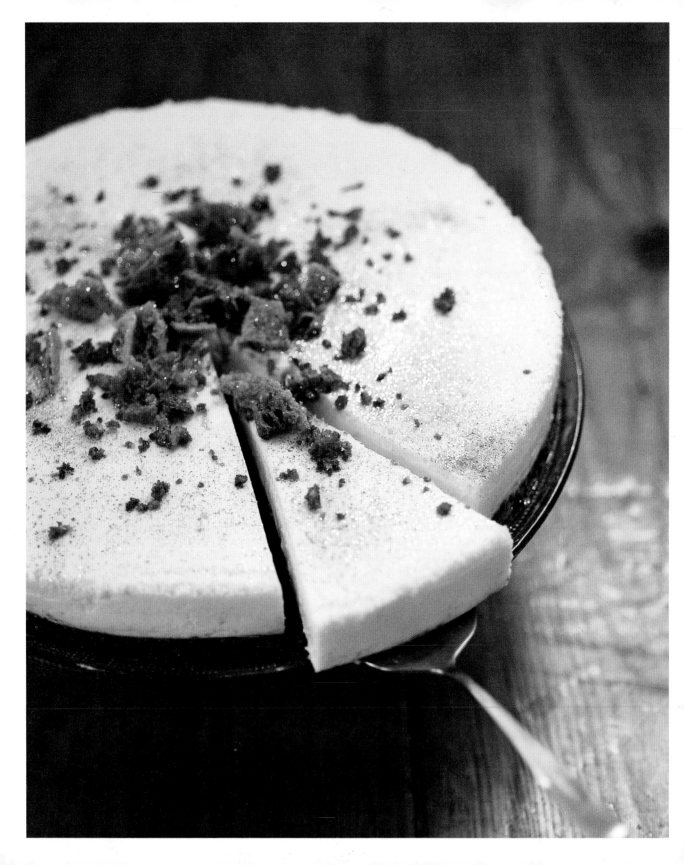

Fridge-Set Honeycomb Cheesecake

The most exciting part of this cheesecake for me was making the honeycomb. Others mightn't be as excited as me, and may decide to simply go out and buy five Crunchies. That's grand. This is a fridge-set cheesecake, which means it's not baked. The setting agent I've used is gelatine, but it isn't suitable for vegetarians, seeing as it's made from cow's hoof or something equally unthinkable. So something else will have to be used. Agar-agar is a word I hear bandied about, but I'm afraid I don't know much about it.

Serves 10

For the base

200g home-made honey-
   comb (which I'll get to)

50g milk chocolate

75g butter

OR

5 Crunchie bars

75g butter

For the honeycomb

4 tablespoons golden syrup

170g caster sugar

3 teaspoons bicarbonate
   of soda

For the filling

200g mascarpone cheese

200g Philadelphia cheese

50g golden caster sugar

150ml condensed milk

1 teaspoon vanilla extract

150ml whipping cream

2 sachets of powdered
   gelatine

To decorate

edible gold glitter (optional)

To make the honeycomb, grease a 20cm square tin. Put the golden syrup, 1 tablespoon water and the sugar into a saucepan. Start on a low heat, until the sugar dissolves, then increase. Stir hard. It will really put up a fight at the beginning. Eventually, as it heats up, it will soften. Bring it to the boil, but watch it like a hawk because sugar is notorious for burning. Bring it down to a simmer for 5 to 10 minutes, then, add the bicarbonate of soda and the honeycomb will start foaming like a rabid dog. Stir, for the love of God, stir! The setting process has already started and you're fighting against time to get all the bicarb through before it goes hard. Mix thoroughly, or as thoroughly as you can, and don't get even an atom of it on your skin because this stuff is like napalm.

Pour into your tin, striving for a fairly even height and shape, but it won't be easy. Never mind, you will get to thump it with a mallet later for its misbehaviour. It should set in around half an hour, but if it stays sticky and tacky, rather than brittle, put it in the fridge. Block out the rest of your evening in order to wash your saucepan.

To make the base, grease a 23cm springform tin. If you're using your home-made honeycomb, put it in a plastic bag and shatter it with a mallet (reserve a little for decorating). Melt the chocolate and butter, mix with the honeycomb, then pack into the bottom of the tin and refrigerate for about an hour. Or, if you're using shop-bought Crunchies, put them in a plastic bag and bash them to smithereens. Keep approximately one-fifth aside for decorating at the end. Melt the butter, mix with four-fifths of the Crunchies, then pack them into the prepared tin and refrigerate for about an hour. To make the filling, beat the mascarpone, Philadelphia, sugar, condensed milk and vanilla extract. In a separate bowl, beat the cream until it's stiff. Fold the cream into the cheese and sugar mix.

Prepare the gelatine by pouring 240ml hot (but not boiling) water into a bowl, then sprinkling the powder on top of the water – the powder always goes into the water, not the other way round. Whisk briskly and for ages – you'll be good and bored – until it's dissolved. Then add it very slowly to the cream/cheese mix. Pour it on top of the set honeycomb base and put in the fridge overnight. Serve with the reserved broken honeycomb and golden glitter sprinkled over the top.

Upside-Down Saffron, Mint and Pomegranate Cheesecake

Upside-down cheesecakes are really having a moment and it's good to be able to chat knowledgeably about them should they crop up in fashionable conversation, right? Let me guide you through my experience.

The biscuit 'base' (which will now be on top) can't be as thick as it usually is because the cheesecake will collapse under the weight. So I decided to dispense with biscuits altogether and used chopped pistachio nuts instead, which give a gorgeous crunch and a beautiful colour. Also, if you normally top your cheesecake with fruit, you have total control over it. But in this case because the fruit is going *underneath* the cheesecake mix, it will get cooked and will change during the process. With some fruit (rhubarb, for example) that's a good thing. But, going for a vaguely Middle Eastern theme, I chose pomegranates, visualizing a carpet of ruby-bright red kernels. And in fairness, that's *exactly* what it looked like when I lined the pie dish with them. But by the end of the baking process, they'd gone a pale pink, almost salmony colour, which wasn't what I wanted. It still tasted delicious, no harm done, I'm only saying.

Finally, the cheesecake itself didn't set as much as other baked cheesecakes I've made. It became like a thick custard, especially towards the middle, so the best way to serve it is to treat it almost like a trifle. Scoop it out with a big serving spoon, rather than trying to cut it into slices. I realize I might have made this sound like a less than joyous experience, but really it was the opposite. The finished product was a triumph. The subtle strangeness of the saffron worked so well with the sharpness of the mint, and the crunchy sweetness of the pistachio nuts went beautifully with the tang of the pomegranate.

Serves 8–10 people

Pinch of saffron threads

200g pomegranate kernels

475g mascarpone cheese

2 eggs

60ml sour cream

125g caster sugar

2–3 capfuls of mint essence

50g plain flour

100g shelled pistachio nuts, chopped roughly

I used a 1 litre pie dish, rather than the baking tin I'd usually go for. There's no need to grease it. Preheat the oven to 160°C/325°F/gas 3.

Dissolve the pinch of saffron threads in 2 tablespoons of cold water and put to one side. Line the base of your pie dish with your beautiful ruby-red pomegranate kernels. Take a moment to savour their jewel-bright redness because the next time you see them, they'll be a far humbler, more apologetic colour.

Beat together the mascarpone, eggs, sour cream, sugar and mint essence until all the lumps are gone. Add the saffron and the water it was dissolved in – the mix will go a beautiful yellow colour. Sieve in the flour and fold through.

Spread the mix over the pomegranate kernels, trying not to disturb them, if you know what I mean. Try to keep them lining the bottom of the dish, while smoothing the top of the cheesecake mix to a roughly level finish. But no need to get neurotic about it. Bake for approximately 50 minutes. For the last 20 minutes of cooking, sprinkle the chopped pistachios over.

LIQUID CAKES

Espresso and Walnut Cake

Three Milks Cake (aka A Hug in a Cake)

Rita-Anne's Birthday Cola Cake

Brazilian Stout Cake

Green Tea Panna Cotta

Zaga's Honey Cake

Barmbrack

Coconut Milk Cake

Not cakes that are actually **LIQUID**, but are made with liquid. I've used a lovely variety here – coffee, milk, cola, stout, honey and various teas – and all give interesting, delicious results. One thing to bring to your attention is that I've included a panna cotta recipe here, which, strictly speaking, isn't 'cake', but is so delicious I hope you'll overlook my tampering with definitions.

Espresso and Walnut Cake

People either love coffee cake or hate it. So some people will be thrilled if you make this for them and others will be less pleased, but for those who like coffee cake, this is a top-notch manifestation of the breed. The walnuts, well, what can I say? My dislike of them is already on the record. I will say no more, but they do go together very well with coffee.

Serves 8

For the cake
50g butter
80ml full-fat milk
1 cup of espresso, cooled
2 eggs
225g caster sugar
100ml sunflower oil
100g walnuts, chopped
250g self-raising flour

For the icing
100g butter
200g icing sugar
1 tablespoon instant coffee*
  dissolved in 1 tablespoon
  boiling water, then cooled
9 walnut halves

*Or instant espresso,
  there is such a thing.

Preheat the oven to 180°C/350°F/gas 4 and grease two 20cm tins.

In a pan, melt the butter and stir in the milk and espresso. In a bowl, whisk the eggs and sugar until foamy, then add the butter/coffee mix and the sunflower oil. Add the chopped nuts, then fold in the flour.

Divide the mix between the two tins and bake for approximately 25 minutes. Do your Skewer Test (see page 23). Cool on a wire tray and turn out of the tins.

Make the icing by whisking the butter with the icing sugar and the dissolved coffee. Use half of the icing to sandwich the two cakes together and spread the other half on top of the cake. Decorate with walnut halves.

Three Milks Cake (aka A Hug in a Cake)

This is the perfect cake for when you've had a bad shock. Say, like your electricity bill arriving after a hard winter or your credit card bill showing up after a mighty shoe binge. This is a lovely cake – sweet and solid and very comforting. I'd be the first to admit that it doesn't look exciting, and as far as complexity of flavour goes (mere vanilla), it doesn't taste wildly exciting either. But cakes don't always need to be exciting. This is a humble, uncomplicated cake, a very loving cake. If a cake could be described as *kind*, then this is it.

What makes this ordinary cake into something extraordinary is the 'three milks'. A fairly ordinary sponge is soaked in the mix for at least 12 hours, totally transforming the texture and density so that every mouthful is sweet and intense. So what I'm trying to say is, plan ahead. If you know a bad bill is coming on a particular date, make this cake the day before.

Serves 9

200g butter

200g caster sugar

4 eggs

200ml sour cream

Seeds of 1 vanilla pod or
  2 teaspoons vanilla extract

200g self-raising flour

½ teaspoon bicarbonate
  of soda

The three milks

200ml evaporated milk

200ml sweetened condensed
  milk

200ml double cream

Preheat the oven to 180°C/350°F/gas 4 and grease a 20cm square loose-bottomed tin.

Cream the butter and sugar until pale and fluffy. Add two of the eggs and half of the sour cream and beat well. Add the other two eggs and the rest of the sour cream and beat again. Add the vanilla flavouring, using whichever method you've decided on. Sieve in the flour and bicarbonate of soda and fold into the mix.

Pile into the prepared tin and bake for approximately 25 minutes, or until a skewer inserted into the middle comes out clean (see page 23).

Cool on a tray until it's fully cold, but don't take the cake out of the tin. Prick the cake surface several times with a fork. Then – bear with me here, I'll try not to make this sound too complicated – wrap the base of the tin with clingfilm. What you're trying to do is liquid-proof the tin. Any moment now you'll be pouring in the three milks and you don't want the liquid leaking down the inside of the tin, out through the loose bottom and into your fridge.

Mix the evaporated milk, condensed milk and cream in a jug, then pour it on top of the cake. Most of the liquid will just 'sit' on the surface of the cake, but don't be alarmed. Put it in the fridge and over the course of several hours a lot of it will be absorbed.

My experiences with this cake have varied – sometimes nearly all of the milk has disappeared, but other times there's still a milky pool sitting there, looking up at me, when I've come to serve it. And the interesting thing is, I've used the exact same quantities every time. If it happens to you that all the liquid doesn't get absorbed, please don't panic, *at all*. Just take a little more care getting it out of the tin, perhaps even using a big serving spoon instead of a knife.

Rita-Anne's Birthday Cola Cake

It was my little sis Rita-Anne's birthday and I decided to make her a cake. I had a good long think about what she likes best (Hula Hoops), and I wasn't sure I'd be able to successfully incorporate them into a cake. Then I remembered that she likes cola almost as much as Hula Hoops, so I made this and she was delighted.

Serves 12–14

225g butter, at room temperature

290g brown soft sugar

2 eggs

2 teaspoons vanilla extract

250ml cola*

125ml buttermilk

250g self-raising flour

30g cocoa powder

1 teaspoon bicarbonate of soda

200g mini marshmallows

For the icing

90ml cola

110g butter

3 tablespoons cocoa powder

250g icing sugar

a bag of fizzy cola bottles (optional)

* Any brand will do, but it must be full-fat, you need the sugar from it.

Preheat the oven to 180°C/350°F/gas 4. Grease and line a big baking tray, 30cm by 23cm and 5cm deep, with baking paper. If you're thinking that this is a BIG cake, big and flat, you're right. It's called a 'sheet' cake.

Beat the butter with the sugar until creamy. Add the eggs and vanilla extract. Mix the cola and buttermilk together in a jug. In a bowl, mix the flour, cocoa powder and bicarbonate of soda together.

Pour about a third of the cola and buttermilk mixture into the creamed butter and sugar, then sieve in about a third of the flour/cocoa/soda mix and stir well. Add another third of the liquid, then another third of the flour and stir again. Go again and it'll all be in. When it's blended and smooth, stir in the marshmallows.

Pour into your – frankly, massive-looking - baking tray and bake for about 35 to 40 minutes. Do the Skewer Test (see page 23). One thing to note, during the baking process the marshmallows will melt, causing small craters to appear in your cake. This is *fine*, you have done nothing wrong. The melted marshmallows will regroup into little, dense, sticky spots of deliciousness, popping up unexpectedly and giving texture and surprise.

Cool the cake on a rack, then extract it from the tray. Proceed with caution because the cake is so big and unwieldy.

To make the icing, put the cola, butter and cocoa powder into a largish saucepan until the butter is melted. Bring to the boil, stirring constantly. Take off the heat, sieve in the icing sugar and whisk like mad. Give this everything you've got because even when you think all of the icing sugar is incorporated, I can assure you it isn't. Stubborn little cysts of it will hold out for an *astonishingly* long time. As the renegade lumps are reluctantly flushed out, the icing will thicken. Eventually you can stop. Let it cool and thicken a little.

If you like, you can simply spread the icing over the cake as it is, in all its enormous, never-ending, prairie-like glory. Or you can cut the cake in half and stack one piece on top of the other, sandwiching them with half the icing, then spreading the remaining icing over the top and sides. Finally, decorate with fizzy cola bottles.

Brazilian Stout Cake

Have you been to Brazil? It's the most wonderful place, with the loveliest people, and I loved the food so much that I bought myself a Brazilian cook book (called, with admirable straightforwardness, *Brazilian Cookery*). I was particularly interested in the cake recipes, but there were some I couldn't make because the ingredients were so exotic – manioc root, anyone? – but this one, with its main ingredient of stout, i.e. Guinness (or similar brand), couldn't have been easier.

I'll address your reservations right now by saying, don't worry about the Guinness. You don't really taste it at all, you just get an intriguing, dark undertow. Also, the alcohol evaporates so it's okay to give it to everyone.

I used lemon buttercream icing and found its sharpness cut through the malty, molassesy cake with flair and aplomb.

You'll notice in the photo that this cake has three layers. I only intended to have two layers, but I accidentally poured far more cake mix into one tin than the other, so that one cake layer ended up almost twice as thick as the other. It was all a bit embarrassing until Himself came up with the idea of slicing the big piece in half horizontally, giving me three layers, almost all the same size. If you also want to go for the three layers, consider doubling the icing.

Serves 12–14

110g butter
85g brown sugar
4 eggs, separated
½ teaspoon ground ginger
1 teaspoon ground cinnamon
1 teaspoon mace*
1 tablespoon grated lemon zest
280g plain flour
½ teaspoon salt
1 tablespoon baking powder
250ml stout
190ml molasses
1 teaspoon bicarbonate of soda

For the icing
150g butter
300g icing sugar
1 teaspoon lemon juice
yellow food colouring (optional)

Preheat the oven to 180°C/350°F/gas 4 and grease two 23cm cake tins.

Cream the butter and sugar. Beat the egg yolks with the ginger, cinnamon, mace and lemon zest. Add to the butter/sugar mix. In a bowl, mix the flour, salt and baking powder together.

Heat the beer to lukewarm and mix in the molasses and bicarbonate of soda. Sift a third of the flour mix into the eggs/butter/sugar, then a third of the beer/molasses. Combine well. Add another third of each and stir again. Add the final third.

Stiffly beat the egg whites and fold into the mix. Divide – equally! – between your two tins. Bake for 35 minutes. Do the Skewer Test (see page 23) then turn out of the tins on to wire racks. Leave to cool.

Make the icing by creaming together the butter and sugar, then adding the lemon juice and enough food colouring until you get your desired yellowness. Use the icing to sandwich the cake layers together, then spread over the top of the cake and down the sides.

*Not the stuff you spray in muggers' eyes. It might sound strange and scary, but it's from the same plant as nutmeg.

Green Tea Panna Cotta

Panna Cotta (Italian for 'cooked cream') is the simplest, most delicious thing ever. The ingredients are basically cream, milk, sugar, flavouring and a setting agent. As with the Fridge-Set Honeycomb Cheesecake recipe on page 91, the setting agent I've used is gelatine, which isn't suitable for vegetarians. My apologies for that, but I believe agar-agar will fit your needs.

However, what I really want to talk to you about is the flavouring. People baulked a little when I told them what they were getting – green tea seems to have a fairly joyless rep – but they became a lot more enthusiastic and animated when I withheld the info about the flavouring. These panna cotta really taste amazing – subtle, delicate, intriguing and delightful.

It seems to be the done thing to make panna cotta in small individual containers. I'm the lucky owner of four adorable little silicone moulds that look like old-fashioned blancmanges. But you can use anything really – ramekins, cups, square sauce bowls, disposable plastic glasses that you get wine in at office leaving parties, etc. – so long as they have a capacity of about 200ml to 250ml.

Serves 4

600ml double cream

150ml full-fat milk

150g caster sugar

12 green tea bags

1 sachet of Dr. Oetker's gelatine

edible glitter (optional)

In a heavy saucepan, bring the cream, milk and sugar to the boil and keep it boiling for about 4 minutes. Lower the temperature, add the tea bags and simmer for 2 to 3 minutes, stirring regularly.

Take the saucepan off the heat and leave to cool for about 5 minutes – it's important that the liquid is below boiling point when you add the gelatine. Remove the teabags and discard them. Then, whisking very briskly with a hand whisk, add the sachet of powdered gelatine. Remember that the powder always gets poured on top of the liquid, never the other way round, and make sure that the gelatine is fully dissolved – this could take a good few minutes of tedious whisking – before you proceed to the next stage. Pour the mixture into the moulds and leave to set in the fridge for at least 3 hours.

To be quite honest, the trickiest part of making this beautiful dessert is getting it out. What I do is I run a little hot water over the bottom of each mould, then gently run the tip of a small sharp knife completely around the edge of the mould, just a few millimetres below the surface. I patiently ease the panna cotta away from the sides and when I feel I can't go any further without breaking the panna cotta, I upend the mould on to the serving bowl and – again more patience required, and I'm so bad at it – 'peel' the mould off.

If you're not using a flexible mould, a tip I got from the interweb is to slide your small sharp knife down as far as you can and simultaneously tip the mould on to its side over the serving dish. Apparently the knife down the side creates an air pocket and helps the panna cotta pop right out on to the dish.

Another extra-special handy hint I came across is to have a droplet of water in the middle of your serving bowl or plate so that if your panna cotta comes out and lands off-centre, you can slide it around until it's centred.

Zaga's Honey Cake

Zaga is mother-in-law to my brother Niall, who is married to Zaga's daughter Ljiljana. Zaga lives in Belgrade and is an AMAZING cook, producing absolute feasts from a (Christ, I hope she won't mind me saying this) tiny kitchen. This cake is straightforward, simple and delicious.

My instinct is always to add tons of spicing and flavouring (often to the point where people choke), but there's no need here, the honey is flavoury enough. Indeed, did you know that the kind of honey you use will influence the taste? I'd always thought honey was just honey, but not at all, there's a universe of different kinds out there. Apparently, it all depends on the kinds of flowers the bees are getting their pollen from. Isn't nature amazing?

Makes 16 cubes

5 eggs, separated

100g caster sugar

100ml oil (sunflower, walnut or hazelnut, if you can get it)

100ml honey

200g plain flour

2 teaspoons baking powder

50g nuts (walnuts, almonds, hazelnuts), finely chopped*

To decorate

edible gold shimmer (optional)

*Feel free to use whatever you like – I used hazelnuts.

Preheat the oven to 200°C/400°F/gas 6 and prepare a 20cm square tin by brushing with oil, then dusting with flour.

Beat the egg yolks with the sugar, then add the oil, honey, flour, baking powder and nuts. In a separate bowl, beat the egg whites until stiff. Mix the two lots together – the yolk mixture will be quite stiff and resistant and the challenge is to fold in the egg whites without knocking all the air out. Do your best, but don't wreck your head.

Pour the mix into your prepared tin, put into the oven and reduce the temperature to 180°C/350°F/gas 4. Bake for 25 to 30 minutes or until a skewer comes out clean.

Cool on a rack, then cut into cubes. If you'd like, you can brush with edible gold shimmer, but there's no need to do anything if you don't want. These little cubes look quite innocuous, but they're lovely. The honey flavour comes as an excellent surprise.

Barmbrack

I'm fairly sure this is an Irish thing. It's traditionally served as a Hallowe'en sweetmeat, but you won't be arrested if you serve it at another time of the year. Except for the month of May. (I joke, of course.)

Basically Barmbrack is a simple loaf cake where the main ingredient is black tea, but with a charming twist – little 'gifts' are dotted in it at random. Common examples are a ring, a key, a coin and a small piece of wood. (The idea goes that if you get the ring in your slice you'll be getting married; a key means a new home or maybe a new car; cracking your tooth on the coin indicates that you'll be coming into money, which will come in handy for paying the dentist; and if you end up with the stick, it means that you'll remain a spinster – delightful.)

Feel free to improvise with your own 'surprises' – for example, I've sometimes added a Berocca tablet to guarantee good health; hair clips to ward off male pattern baldness; or a tiny little shoe to predict ... er ... well, new shoes. But for the love of God, wrap each 'surprise' in a big lump of tinfoil, to make them unmissably visible so that no-one accidentally swallows them. People have gone terrible litigious.

Serves 8–10

170g light brown soft sugar
85g sultanas
85g raisins
40g mixed peel
450ml black tea, cooled
160g self-raising flour
1 level teaspoon bicarbonate
of soda
1 egg, beaten

Put the sugar, fruit, peel and tea in a bowl. Leave to soak overnight.

On the day itself, grease a 1lb (450g) loaf tin and line it with baking paper OR save yourself all that trouble and use a silicone loaf tin. Preheat the oven to 170°C/325°F/gas 3.

Sift the flour and bicarbonate of soda into the tea/sugar/fruit stew, then add the beaten egg and stir well.

Pour into your loaf tin, then 'plant' your little surprises at regular intervals into the mix so that each slice will contain something and you don't have anyone boohoohooing and bellyaching and saying that they didn't get anything and that their younger brother is going to be getting a Ferrari and why do they never get anything and why is life so unfair. Make sure that each piece of tinfoil is fully immersed in the cake mix because if it's sticking up into the open air, it might burn. Bake for 1 hour and 35 minutes or do your Skewer Test (see page 23).

Leave for 5 minutes, then turn out on to a wire rack. Cut into slices and serve with plenty of butter. Because of the foil-wrapped surprises, this is a very sociable cake, one of the few that I like to share with others. (In a perfect universe, I'd prefer to eat cake alone, in a darkened room, answerable to no one, slice after slice. And when it's all gone, I'd brush off any incriminating crumbs, fold the box into very small pieces, stash it in the bottom of the bin and deny that there had ever been any baked goods in the house at all.)

Coconut Milk Cake

This is a direct transcript of a text I got from my beloved friend Judy a couple of hours after I dropped some Coconut Milk Cake over to herself and her husband Fergal. 'OMG Marian! Ure cake! Nearly all gone! Had huge slice after seeing Fergal's orgasmic face as he had a piece. It's d most scrumptious, deliciously moist cake I ever tasted!'…ahem…modest cough. Speaks for itself, no?

A couple of things. Don't worry if you can't get hold of any dried shredded coconut. You can substitute desiccated if you prefer, or you can leave it out altogether. Also, if you do manage to get hold of some dried shredded coconut, don't be alarmed if the pieces remind you of dried toenail clippings – they will soften and change during the baking process.

Now, the syrup. It's not vital. It's just that it makes it all even more coconutty and moist and fabulous. Anyway, as most of the coconut milk I encounter comes in 400ml cans, it seemed like a good way of using up the leftovers from the cake.

Makes 20 to 26 slices – yes, this is a BIG cake

170g butter
300g caster sugar
4 eggs
1 tablespoon vanilla extract
250g self-raising flour
pinch of salt
¾ teaspoon baking powder
50g dried shredded coconut
200ml coconut milk

For the (optional) syrup
200ml coconut milk
40g light brown soft sugar

Preheat the oven to 170°C/325°F/gas 3 and liberally butter the inside of a 25cm bundt pan.

Beat the butter and sugar together until pale and fluffy. Add the eggs, one at a time, mixing well between each addition. Add the vanilla extract. In a separate bowl, mix together the sieved flour, salt, baking powder and shredded coconut.

Pour about a third of the coconut milk and a third of the flour mix into the butter/sugar/eggs and beat well. Add another third of coconut milk and flour and mix well. Then add the final amount. Doing it in this stop-start fashion might be slightly irritating, but will prevent lumps from forming. Pour the mix into the pan and bake for 1 hour.

Cool on a wire rack, then, still keeping the cake in the tin, prick its surface with a fork many, many times – will we agree on twenty?

Make the syrup by gently heating the coconut milk and sugar together until the sugar dissolves. Pour about half of the syrup over the cake (still in its tin) and let it trickle through the fork holes into the 'body' of the cake. After a couple of hours, pour the rest over.

Give the cake plenty of time to absorb the syrup – I'd recommend leaving it overnight – then be very careful taking it out of the tin because it will be quite moist, especially if you've gone the syrup route. Finally, cut into slices and serve to your loved ones. Prepare yourself for ecstatic texts.

PASTRY

Mini Key Lime Pies

Mam's Apple Tart

Pecan Pie

Pear and Hazelnut Flan

Chocolate Hazelnut Torte

Profiteroles

Puff Pastry Pineapple 'Tarte Tatin'

Lemon Curd and Pistachio Pinwheels

Chocolate Baklava

PASTRY. Scares the life out of people. Almost as bad as meringues. But don't be afraid. I'll hold your hand through this.

Nearly all the recipes I'll take you through are versions of shortcrust pastry – I've started with a basic recipe and become progressively more ambitious and fancy. (There is a short, terrifying detour, where we'll veer wildly off track and do choux pastry, but then we'll return to the path.) We're going to make a couple of dishes using puff pastry and filo pastry, but we're not even going to attempt to make the pastry because everyone – even, I'm reliably informed, professional chefs – buys the pre-made stuff. If they cannot be bothered to make it from scratch, I don't see why we should put ourselves through it. There is no shame in this.

The key to good shortcrust pastry is to keep everything as cold as possible. Professional bakers make their pastry in the morning, before the kitchen heats up. I mean, that's the level of sensitivity we're dealing with here.

Most of the recipes I'm giving you here are pie *bases*, so the pastry is playing a mere supporting part, rather than a leading role. Just a quick note – I've baked them in pie tins or dishes rather than cake tins. They're very similar but with a pie dish or tin the side will gently slope outwards. Sometimes the sides will be 'fluted', which means frilly. Also – sorry to bamboozle you with details – pie dishes come in different depths. Shallow ones are about 3cm deep and deeper ones can be 5cm deep, but I'm only using shallow ones in this section.

Mini Key Lime Pies

These little beauties are made with a basic shortcrust pastry, as basic as it gets. It's basically flour, butter and water, nothing to scare the horses.

In keeping with this gentle introduction, these pies are small, which means there's less surface area of pastry to grapple with, which, trust me, helps a lot.

Just one thing, these need to be refrigerated for at least 6 hours, so plan ahead.

Makes 4 mini pies

For the basic shortcrust pastry

170g plain flour

pinch of salt

100g butter, chilled and cut into cubes

For the filling

4 egg yolks

400ml sweetened condensed milk

juice of 6 limes

To decorate

edible glitter and lime slices (optional)

For these pies, I use 4 silicone moulds, 11cm wide. Because I use silicone moulds, there's no need to grease them. But if you're using metal tins, butter liberally.

There are a couple of ways we can make shortcrust pastry – by hand or by machine. In the next recipe I'll tell you the food processor method, but here I'm going to tell you how to make pastry by hand. You might think, For the love of God, I've got a busy life, I've better things to be doing than making pastry by hand! Or you might think, I'm going out of my mind here, give me some sort of small, soothing task. And really, this is as small and soothing as it gets.

Sieve the flour and salt into a bowl, then add the cubed butter. Using the tips of your fingers, start rubbing small pieces of butter and small pieces of flour together. As you do, lift your hands into the air above the bowl and let the stuff fall back in. Eventually – but it'll take a while – the mix will begin to resemble fine breadcrumbs.

Don't try to speed this up. If you do it too quickly, the butter will become greasy and your pastry won't be as crisp. So slow down. Embrace the process. Think of it as meditation for your fingers.

Remember what I said about coldness. Think about Lapland. Blizzards. Frostbite.

Keep rubbing and lifting and breathing and feeling your feet on the ground and when you feel the flour and butter have become as one, add a tablespoon of cold water and – mark me carefully here – stir it in using a knife. Yes, a knife. I had always been told that it was bad luck to stir anything with a knife, but now I feel there's no such thing as good or bad luck, life is simply life and we can't ward off bad stuff by saluting magpies or lighting candles or refusing to stir things with knives. Whatever is going to happen is going to happen, so stir away. The knife will keep things cold, so even if the roof falls in, your pastry will be nice. •••

The mix will start to cohere, by that I mean it'll start sticking together and looking like pastry. If you need to add another tablespoon of water, do, but easy does it, you don't want your pastry to become tacky. Use your hands for the final 'bringing together.'

Pat it into a flat round, cover in clingfilm and put in the fridge for at least an hour.

Now it's time to roll out your pastry and there are a couple of ways we can do this. We'll do the Floured Surface Version here and I'll tell you the Clingfilm Method in the next recipe.

First, preheat the oven to 170°C/325°F/gas 3.

Remove the clingfilm and with a sharp knife, cut the pastry into quarters.

Dust a clean surface with plain flour and place one of the quarters of pastry in the middle of it. Also dust your rolling pin with flour (unless you have a non-stick silicone one) and with firm, confident strokes, flatten and 'stretch' the pastry, so that it becomes more of an oval shape. Shift the pastry 90 degrees so that now it's wide and short. Sweep a fresh layer of flour under the pastry because otherwise it will stick to the surface and it'll be a nightmare. Roll again and now you'll have more of a round shape. Keep shifting the pastry 90 degrees, keep sweeping fresh flour under the pastry and keep rolling, until the dough is big enough and roughly the right shape to line the bottom and sides of one of your moulds. This shouldn't take long because the moulds are only small and it'll be a different story when we're dealing with full-sized pies, but let's not worry about that now.

Trim the edge of the pastry with a sharp knife and bake the pastry blind for 15 minutes (see page 21).

To make the filling, whisk the egg yolks until they go a little pale. Add in the condensed milk and the juice of the 6 limes, then whisk again. Divide the mix among the four partially baked pastry cases and bake for 15 minutes.

Cool on a wire rack and refrigerate for at least 6 hours.

If you're in the mood, decorate with glitter and other stuff, but they're just as wonderful served plain.

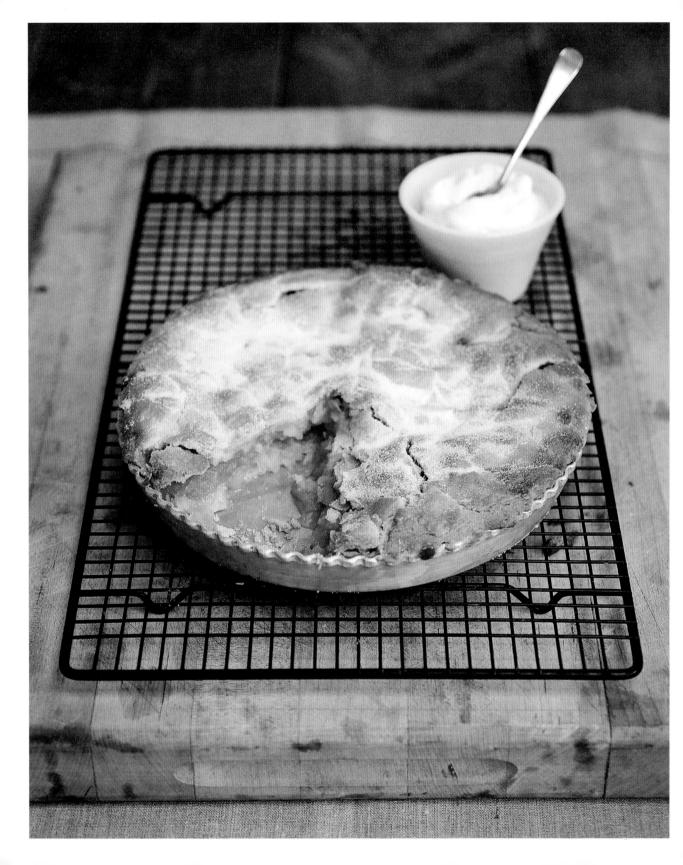

Mam's Apple Tart

Mam is my beloved mother. A famously reluctant cook, she was, however, a dab hand at the apple tarts, and could make them in her sleep. This is utterly delicious and brought memories of childhood rushing back.

Serves 6

For the pastry

170g plain flour

55g icing sugar

110g butter, chilled and cut into cubes

1 egg yolk

For the filling

5 cooking apples, peeled, cored and chopped

4 cloves and 1 cinnamon stick*

2 tablespoons caster sugar

For the glaze

1 egg, lightly beaten (or milk)

caster sugar

*Obviously my mother didn't use such stuff. Any Irish woman found adding flavouring to food in the 1960s could have been stripped of her citizenship.

Grease a 20cm pie tin.

You can make this pastry in your food processor if you're lucky enough to have one. (If not, see the instructions in the previous recipe for making pastry by hand.) Sieve the flour and icing sugar together, then add the butter. Beat slowly until the mix goes sandy and there are no lumps of butter still visible. Add the egg yolk and mix again. The pastry should gradually cohere, i.e. start looking like pastry. If it still looks dry and crumbly (this is unlikely) add a tablespoon of cold water and mix again.

Wrap the lump of pastry in clingfilm, then put in the fridge for at least an hour.

Meanwhile, put the chopped cooking apples into a heavy-bottomed saucepan. (To be quite honest, I didn't know you could even *get* cooking apples any more. I thought they were something from the olden days.)

Bash the cloves (this releases their oil) and add to the apples along with the cinnamon stick. Add the caster sugar and 2 tablespoons water and stew over a gentle heat. However, to quote Mam here, 'Go aisy! You don't want the apples to turn to mush.'

When the apples are soft but still lumpy – this should take about 20 minutes – test for sweetness. If you think they're a bit sour, add more sugar.

Preheat the oven to 170°C/325°F/gas 3.

Now, for the Clingfilm Method of rolling out pastry. Take the pastry out of the fridge and remove the clingfilm. Divide the pastry into two 'halves', one slightly bigger than the other. Shape the bigger half into a round, then place on a piece of clingfilm, about 30cm by 30cm. Place another piece of clingfilm – roughly the same size as the first one – on top of the pastry, then use your rolling pin to flatten the pastry. To confirm, your pastry is enveloped between both pieces of clingfilm and your rolling pin is rolling over the top piece. I'm sorry if this is confusing. The thing is, it's actually a useful thing to get the hang of because the clingfilm will 'hold' the pastry so that it's less likely to break as you roll it out. •••

So roll the pastry, then turn the whole clingfilmed parcel 90 degrees and roll again, and so on, until your pastry is roughly the right size and shape to line your tin. You might think, Feck this clingfilm malarkey, it's far too much trouble, and if so, then stop. I don't want to add to your woes, only reduce them.

Right, now the tricky bit, getting the pastry into the tin. Remove the top layer of clingfilm. Place your rolling pin horizontally across the dough and using it almost as a hinge, fold the pastry in two and lift it off the bottom layer of clingfilm – do this *very* quickly, this is not a time to start staring thoughtfully into the distance and musing on existential matters – then lower it into the tin.

Things might go pear-shaped on you – they did for me, my pastry 'broke' – but don't panic. What I did was assemble a 'patchwork' pastry case. I put the biggest unbroken piece into the tin, then used the next-biggest piece to cover more of the tin, overlapping the joins slightly. I kept doing this until the tin was fully lined, then I pressed my fingers along the joins until they had all but disappeared.

Even if your pastry doesn't fully break, holes may develop and there's no shame in this, no shame at all. Just patch the holes with more pastry and move on.

Trim the edges with a sharp knife, then add in the stewed apple. Yes, that's right, no baking blind on this tart. Mam sounded *extremely* surprised when I suggested it. She's never done it – probably because she was so busy – but the tarts never suffered. It means that the bottom layer of pastry stays soft and crumbly, instead of crunchy, but no less delicious for it.

Roll out the second 'half' of pastry using whichever method appeals to you, then drape it over the top of the tart. Stick the edge of the bottom layer against the edge of the top layer, using the egg wash or milk.

Swipe the top layer with the egg wash or milk and prick several times with a fork. Bake for about 30 minutes, until the pastry is golden brown.

Scatter caster sugar over the top just before serving.

Pecan Pie

Now, *this* is a magnificent creation. It's a pastry base, with a pecan nut and golden syrup filling, topped off by serried ranks of perfect pecans, made extra beautiful-looking with the addition of a glaze.

Serves 10

For the pastry

225g plain flour

pinch of salt

55g lard, chilled and
  cut into cubes*

85g butter, chilled and cut
  into cubes

2 teaspoons caster sugar

For the filling

400g pecan nuts

3 eggs

200g light brown soft sugar

150ml golden syrup

50g butter, melted

1 teaspoon vanilla extract

2 tablespoons plain flour

For the (optional) glaze

2 tablespoons pear/apple
  spread**

*I know! Sounds gross, yes?
  But go with it.

**You can get it in health
  food shops.

Grease a 24cm pie tin.

Make the pastry by sieving the flour into a bowl with the salt and rubbing the fat in, either using your hands or your food processor. When the mixture starts to look like fine breadcrumbs, add the sugar. At this stage you might be able to bring the pastry together with your hands. If it still looks a bit crumbly, add a tablespoon of cold water. Now, with this pie, I did something a little unexpected (even to myself). I didn't chill the pastry and then roll it out. I shaped the pastry into a ball, placed it in the centre of the dish and used the heel of my hand to flatten it. I kept pushing and flattening the pastry until it reached the edges of the dish, then encouraged it to climb the sides. In fairness, things got a little lopsided, with one side a bit thicker than the other, but no matter! I simply removed a strip of pastry from the 'fat' side and use it to bulk out the thinner side.

When the entire inside of the tin was lined with pastry, I put it in the fridge for half an hour.

When the half-hour was up, I preheated the oven to 200°C/400°F/ gas 6 and baked the pastry blind for 20 minutes (see page 21). Then I removed the paper and beans and baked it for another 5 minutes.

Meanwhile, I began the filling by segregating the pecan nuts, keeping the handsome, whole ones aside for decorating the top and shunting off the manky, broken ones for inclusion in the mix. I didn't feel good about this pecan nut apartheid and resolved that the next time, the broken ones would be on display.

I whisked the eggs, then added the sugar, golden syrup, melted butter, vanilla extract, sieved flour and reject pecan nuts, stirring well. I poured the mix into the pastry case and arranged the good-looking pecans in an attractive fashion on the top.

At this point, I lowered the oven temperature to 170°C/325°F/gas 3 and baked for about a further 30 minutes. (Cover with a bit of tinfoil if the pecans on top begin to catch.)

While the tart cooled (on a wire rack) I mixed the apple/pear spread with 2 tablespoons of boiling water and microwaved on half-power for 2 minutes, then used a pastry brush to paint the glaze over the top.

Pear and Hazelnut Flan

What makes this flan extra special is the addition of ground hazelnuts into the pastry. It gives an unexpected density of flavour, which goes very nicely with the sweetness of the pears. This flan might seem like a very work-intensive thing because you'll be making custard and a glaze in addition to the pastry, but it's all fairly simple and very worth it.

Serves 10

For the pastry

50g hazelnuts, ground to a fine flour

100g plain flour

pinch of salt

75g butter, chilled and cut into cubes

1 tablespoon caster sugar

1 egg, beaten

For the filling

3 eggs

1 egg yolk

55g caster sugar

1 teaspoon vanilla extract

300ml double cream

3–4 ripe pears, peeled, halved and cored

For the glaze

4 tablespoons apricot jam

Grease a 22cm flan dish.

Make the pastry by mixing the ground nuts, sieved flour and salt, then incorporating the butter using either your fingers or your food processor. When the mix resembles fine breadcrumbs, add the sugar, then make a well in the middle and add the beaten egg. It should start looking like pastry at this stage, but if it's still a bit dry, add a tablespoon of cold water.

Roll the pastry into a ball, wrap in clingfilm and refrigerate for an hour.

When the hour is nearly up, preheat the oven to 180°C/350°F/gas 4. (Any pastry made with nuts needs to be cooked at a slightly lower temperature than plain pastry, because the nuts are more prone to burning.) Roll the pastry out using your preferred method (see page 117 for the Floured Surface version or page 119 for the Clingfilm Method), bake blind for 15 minutes (see page 21), then remove the paper and beans and bake for another 10 minutes.

Meanwhile, make the custard filling by whipping the eggs, the egg yolk, the sugar and the vanilla extract, but not for long, you're not looking for foamy here, just mixed. Scald the cream (see page 21), then *very, very gradually* pour it in to the beaten eggs, whisking all the time. (The reason you add it so gradually is to prevent the heat of the cream scrambling the eggs.)

Pour the custard into your pastry case, then place the pear halves, spaced at equal intervals, into the custard. Back into the oven it goes for another 30 minutes, but keep an eye on it. If the edges of the pastry start to look like they might take a notion to be overcooked – or, God forbid, even burnt – cover the whole thing with a sheet of tinfoil.

Cool on a wire rack and make the glaze by adding a tablespoon of boiling water to the apricot jam, then microwaving on half-power for 2 minutes. Strain the warm jam through a sieve so that the fruity 'bits' get left behind and what goes into your bowl is a sticky liquid.

Use a pastry brush to gently paste the glaze on to the surface of the flan. This makes a HUGE difference to the final look of the flan – it's like the difference between going out without your lipstick on, and with it on. HUGE difference.

Chocolate Hazelnut Torte

We're stepping things up a further notch here by making chocolate pastry. Not as intimidating to make as it might initially sound because the chocolatey-ness is coming from cocoa powder, rather than melted chocolate. The filling, on the other hand, is a stunningly rich, delicious affair. Chocolate and hazelnuts are a great combination and some strange witchcraft happens when you add coffee. Instead of making the torte taste like coffee, it has the effect of making the chocolate taste even more like chocolate. And God knows, that has to be good.

Serves 8

For the chocolate pastry

175g plain flour

50g cocoa powder

½ teaspoon baking powder

50g icing sugar

140g butter, chilled and cut into cubes

3 egg yolks

For the filling

160g dark chocolate (70% cocoa solids)

140g butter

140g caster sugar

140g hazelnuts, ground to a fine flour

4 eggs, separated

30g cocoa powder

1 tablespoon instant coffee, dissolved in 2 tablespoons boiling water, then cooled

Liberally grease a 22cm pie tin with butter, but don't go preheating any oven yet, hold your horses!

Make the pastry by sieving together the flour, cocoa powder and baking powder. Add the icing sugar, then incorporate the butter, either by using your fingers or using your food processor. When it starts to look like fine breadcrumbs, add in the egg yolks. It should become quite sticky at this stage.

Because of its wet consistency, this pastry is quite tricky to handle so my advice is that you don't roll it out with a rolling pin, but that you use the Pressing Method I described on page 122. I promise you it'll make life much easier.

When the tin is fully lined, put in the fridge and chill for at least 20 minutes.

Preheat the oven to 200°C/400°F/gas 6 and bake the pastry blind for 15 minutes (see page 21). Then remove the beans and paper and bake for a further 5 minutes.

Take the pastry out of the oven and reduce the temperature to 160°C/325°F/gas 3.

Now it's time to make the fabulous filling.

Melt the chocolate and butter together in a large heatproof bowl over a saucepan of simmering water.

Remove from the heat and beat in the sugar, ground hazelnuts, egg yolks, cocoa powder and dissolved coffee.

In a separate bowl, beat the egg whites until they're holding soft peaks, then fold into the chocolate mixture.

Pour into the pastry case and bake for 40 minutes — when you take it out, the middle will probably still have a bit of wobble to it, this is all fine — and cool on a wire rack.

Remove with great care from the tin and serve in smallish slices because this is very, very intense and you don't want your guests (or indeed yourself) going into a chocolate coma.

Profiteroles

What we're making here is choux pastry and it's *much* easier than you might think. Much! I really didn't believe I'd be able to make profiteroles in a million years, but I did and they were fantastic. Admittedly a bit bockety shape-wise, but they tasted great.

Makes 15–18

For the pastry
85g butter
½ teaspoon caster sugar
115g plain flour
Pinch of salt
3 medium eggs, beaten

For the cream filling
450ml whipping cream
15g icing sugar

For the chocolate topping
175g dark chocolate
    (70% cocoa solids)
100ml double cream

Lightly oil a large baking tray. Preheat the oven to 200°C/400°F/gas 6.

Place the butter and sugar into a large saucepan with 200ml of water and heat over a low heat until the butter melts. Increase the heat and bring the mixture to the boil, then, quick as a flash, pour all the flour and salt in, in one go.

Remove from the heat and whisk like mad until a smooth paste forms.

When the paste starts curling away from the sides of the pan, whisk in a little of the beaten egg. When that's fully incorporated, add a little more of the egg and whisk again. Continue adding the egg until the mixture is smooth and shiny.

Heat a tablespoon in a jug of warm water, then use it to spoon out a tablespoon of the mix on to the baking tray. Use your finger to 'encourage' the batter off the spoon, then wipe the spoon, warm it in the water and do it all again. Leave a space of at least 5cm between each profiterole because they will puff up and expand while they bake.

Also, while it's admirable to aim to have the profiteroles roughly the same size and shape as each other, please accept that if you're new to this game, you'll end up with an almost shockingly random selection of differently sized, different shaped lumps. Try to forgive their flaws and love them for their uniqueness. (Another heavy-handed aphorism from the Marian Keyes School for Self-Acceptance. My apologies.)

Bake for 25 to 30 minutes. Remove from the oven and prick the base of each pastry ball, then return to the oven, with the hole facing upwards, for 5 more minutes. Remove from the oven and cool on a wire rack.

Make the cream filling by whisking the cream until soft peaks form. Stir in the icing sugar. Slice each profiterole in two horizontally, then sandwich the two halves back together with a tablespoon of the whipped cream.

Make the chocolate topping by melting the chocolate in a heatproof bowl over a pan of simmering water. Add the cream and stir well. Leave to cool and thicken slightly, then spoon generously over the top of each profiterole.

Wait until the chocolate topping has cooled and set. Serve with pride at your achievement.

Puff Pastry Pineapple 'Tarte Tatin'

Puff pastry is the very divil to make. Even professional chefs use pre-made, shop-bought stuff so there's nothing wrong in us doing so either.

This is an homage to the classical tarte tatin, which, if I have my facts right, is an upside-down apple tart. What happens is that you caramelize the apples in a frying pan, then add the pastry (usually shortcrust, I think), bake, then invert on to a plate, so that the apple is on top.

This tart works on the same principle – fruit being caramelized in a frying pan, then pastry draped over it. But what makes this boyo special is the filling. It's a combination of pineapple, black pepper and – brace yourself – dried chilli flakes. It works. It's strange, but it works. But you must be careful because dried chilli flakes are very, very, very hot.

Serves 10

For the filling

75g butter

75g light brown soft sugar

squeeze of lemon juice

450g pineapple chunks – can be tinned or fresh, but must be drained of all juice

pinch of salt

1 teaspoon black pepper

½ teaspoon dried chilli flakes

For the pastry

340g block of ready-made puff pastry*

*Feel free to buy frozen, no shame in that either, but give yourself maybe 3 hours defrosting time.

Preheat the oven to 200°C/400°F/gas 6. In a 22cm (approx.) ovenproof frying pan, over a gentle heat, dissolve the butter, sugar and lemon juice until a caramel forms. Stir continuously with a wooden spoon – this burns in the blink of an eye. Keep stirring, keep stirring. You might become a little bit bored. Think of something nice and keep stirring. Eventually all the sugar will dissolve and you will have a caramel.

Increase the heat a tiny amount and add the pineapple chunks, the salt, black pepper and chilli flakes. Keep stirring. A lot of juice will escape from the pineapple as you cook, so the thick texture of the sauce will change into more of a syrup. This is all okay.

On a floured board, roll out your chunk of – yes! Shop bought! Hold your head up high! – puff pastry, until you have a vaguely circley shape. Because puff pastry (I've found) has a tendency to shrink once it's in the oven, make your circley shape much bigger than your frying pan.

'Gather' your pineapple chunks towards the centre of the frying pan, then drape the pastry over the whole pan, tucking in the excess at the sides. Prick with a fork four or five times.

Bake for 15 minutes at 200°C, then lower the heat to 180°C/350°F/gas 4 and bake for another 15 minutes.

During the baking process, the pastry might 'puff' up (I suppose it feels it has to live up to its name) into a dome-like shape. Simply place a fish slice (or similar device) onto it and push it back down again. The air will leave through the holes you made with the fork at the start and all will be well. It might chance its arm and try puffing up again, but once more simply take your fish slice and flatten it back down. It is not the boss of you.

Remove from the oven, leave to cool fully on a wire rack, then carefully invert on to a serving plate.

Lemon Curd and Pistachio Pinwheels

This is another fabulous recipe where you barefacedly use shop-bought puff pastry.

Makes 16

A packet of 2 sheets of
  frozen ready-made puff
  pastry, total weight 425g*

For the filling
160g lemon curd
160g pistachio nuts,
  chopped roughly

*The ones I bought were
  rectangular sized, 280mm x
  215mm. They came rolled
  up so, while they were still
  frozen, I unrolled them and
  laid them flat. They each
  came on a sheet of plastic
  (blue, if it's of any interest),
  so I just kept them on it
  and didn't have to bother
  with floured boards. I gave
  them about an hour and a
  half to defrost.

Line two baking trays with baking paper and preheat the oven to 220°C/425°F/gas 7.

Spread half of the lemon curd on to the first pastry sheet – it should be a very thin covering, a mere scraping – then scatter over half of the pistachio nuts. Take the short end of the pastry, lift it slightly and start rolling it inwards and over on to itself, as tightly as possible, but not so tightly that the filling starts to squeeze out the sides. (This gets easier with practice, I promise.) Proceed with patience, but confidence, making sure that the rolling is happening evenly across the width of the pastry.

Very soon, it will be all rolled up and you will have a little log.

Repeat the whole process with the second sheet of pastry and the rest of the lemon curd and pistachios.

Use a serrated knife to cut each log into eight equal pieces. You might have to dip the knife in water occasionally because the lemon curd filling may stick to it and make the cutting difficult. Carefully lay each pinwheel flat on your baking trays. Leave plenty of room between them because the pastry will puff and expand.

Bake for about 20 minutes. There might be mild filling leakage from some of the pinwheels, but don't let that bother you. Do watch though that they don't catch on the bottom.

When you take the pinwheels out of the oven, prepare to be amazed. They will look so professional and impressive and totally different from the last time you saw them.

Let them stay on their trays while they cool.

You can recreate this with a million different fillings – Morello cherry jam and chopped hazelnuts, for example. Or lime curd – have you ever had the pleasure? Very hard to get hold of, but oh my God, SO delicious, far nicer than lemon, if you ask me – teamed with chopped macadamia nuts. Let your imagination run wild! But *never* lie about the pastry being shop-bought.

Chocolate Baklava

This is another shame-free recipe using more shop-bought pastry, filo this time. Baklava, though. Cripes, was I intimidated. So intimidated that I had to involve Himself because he has a lot of qualities that I lack – patience, dexterity and patience. Also, he's very patient. (I defensively describe myself as more of an 'ideas' person.) So using our different but symbiotic personalities, we fashioned a Baklava together and I swear to God, we were so proud of the finished product that it was almost like we'd had a baby. We kept taking photos of it, the way people do with newborns.

In one way I was right to be so intimidated – filo pastry is very fragile and large sheets of it are hard to handle without them tearing. But next time I think I could do it on my own. I'll take you through it step-by-step so that you can do this solo if you want.

The Nutella was my idea (did I mention that I'm an 'ideas' person?).

Makes about 20 baklava, approx. 4cm by 5cm

For the baklava
12 sheets of uncooked and defrosted filo pastry*
250g pistachio nuts
200g walnuts
100g pecan nuts
6 cardamom pods
160g Nutella
175g butter

For the syrup
300g granulated sugar
2 capfuls of rosewater

*The only filo pastry sheets I could find were exactly the right width for my baking tin, but too long. I agonized about what to do with the excess and couldn't come up with a solution, so I'm afraid there was some wastage. You might have better luck finding shorter sheets. Or you might have a longer tin.

You'll be using a 23cm by 30cm baking tin. Preheat the oven to 180°C/350°F/gas 4.

Have the pastry standing by, but keep it covered with a damp cloth as it dries out quickly.

Make the filling by putting all the nuts and the cardamom pods into a food processor and grinding them until they're pretty small. Not complete dust, but say, the size of large breadcrumbs. Move them to a separate bowl, add the Nutella and mix well. Keep standing by.

Melt the butter until it's liquid. Using a pastry brush, paint a lot of melted butter on the base and up the sides of the tin you're using. Then, this is where it could get challenging. Take a sheet of filo pastry and gently lay it on the base of the tin. Carefully brush it with melted butter, then take another length of pastry, lay it on top of the first one and brush with melted butter. Keep going, until you've got six slices of filo pastry, lying one on top of the other, with a layer of melted butter in between each.

Remember, the pastry is very thin and fragile. Himself was in charge of draping and laying and I was in charge of brushing the melted butter and it was fairly intensive work. At one stage Himself said, 'Imagine, if you had to actually *make* the filo pastry as well as all this other stuff.' He had a good think about it and then he muttered, 'God, no *wonder* the Ottoman Empire collapsed.'

When the six layers are in place, spread the nut/cardamom/Nutella evenly over the entire surface. Then it's time to start preparing the 'top' of your baklava. Lay a length of pastry over the nut/Nutella

•••

mix, brush with melted butter, lay down another layer of pastry, again brushing with melted butter, and so on until you've used up all the pastry. (All in all, you should have used twelve sheets of pastry, six underneath the filling and six on top.) Finish with a layer of melted butter.

Then it's time to cut the baklava into shapes – it's easier to do this now than later when they're cooked. It's traditional to serve baklava in diamond shapes and the best way to do this is to first cut the uncooked baklava in the tin into four long, equally sized strips (going right down to the bottom layer of pastry). Then cut diagonal lines – the more lines you cut, the smaller your individual baklava will be. Himself cut approximately five diagonal lines, which ended up giving us twenty pieces, but if you cut more lines, closer to each other, you'll get more – but smaller – cakes.

Bake for 20 minutes, then lower the temperature to 150°C/300°F/gas 2 and cook for another 30 to 40 minutes.

Meanwhile, make the syrup by dissolving the sugar in 275ml water and the rosewater. Stirring constantly, bring it to bubbling point, but make sure it doesn't burn. Leave to cool.

When the baklava comes out of the oven, go over the diagonal cuts again with a sharp knife, then pour the syrup along the 'fault lines'. Leave the baklava to absorb the syrup for a good few hours, overnight if possible. This is a stunningly delicious cake and people simply won't be able to believe that you made it yourself.

MERINGUES AND MACAROONS

Blueberry Mess

Shirley's Ginger and Pineapple Pavlova

Zagina Reforma Torta (Zaga's Reform Chocolate Cake)

Banana Meringue Pie

Basic Cranberry Macaroons

Mango Macaroons

Apple Macaroons

Bluegrass Macaroons

Tiramisu Macaroons

Very Chocolatey Macaroons

People fear **MERINGUES**. They regard the egg white as a slippery customer – unreliable, capricious, even treacherous. And I agree that an egg white has to be handled right. But there is a key to mastering meringues and that key is to be just a little OCD – have your bowl super-clean, have your beaters super-clean (not that they'd be any other way, of course) and separate your eggs with extreme care – don't let even an atom of egg yolk get into the egg whites (which is why I recommend using three bowls, see the tip on page 21). The thing is, that grease of any kind is the enemy of the meringue. I won't bamboozle you with the science, but basically grease *interferes*. It stops the egg whites becoming foamy and thick, so you could be beating until Judgement Day and your egg whites could still be eyeballing you with mulish resistance, refusing to change.

Apparently, there's also a danger of overbeating egg whites and causing the mix to curdle. However, that's never happened to me because I have too short an attention span and get bored long before we reach that point.

The best bowl to make meringues in is copper – a chemical reaction happens that stabilizes the egg whites – but I don't have a copper bowl and I've still managed to produce the goods, so don't stress.

From my experience, there are several versions of meringues and a lot has to do with the temperature and length of time they're baked at. You get meringues that are dry, crunchy, almost chalky. Then there are 'cakey' meringues, which are made with a high quantity of ground nuts. Sometimes meringue is used as a pie topping so that it's golden on the outside but still 'wet' on the inside. Or you can have meringues that are downright chewy, as in **MACAROONS**. They are all fabulous.

Blueberry Mess

A nice easy introduction to meringues, this one. Very simple. It's a variation on the classic Eton Mess, only I've used blueberries instead of strawberries and Greek yoghurt instead of cream. And you don't have to have gone to Eton.

There's very little that can go wrong here. This is a 'dry' meringue, but because it will be broken up into small pieces, it really doesn't matter if you over- or under-bake it. The only tricky thing about this is that the meringue needs to be made the day before you want to eat it.

Serves 4

For the meringue
2 egg whites
120g caster sugar
blue food colouring, the gel type*

For the filling
200–300g blueberries
400g Greek yoghurt
edible blue glitter (optional)**

*I like Squires' Ice Blue or Navy.

**I say optional, but to me it's vital.

Preheat the oven to 140°C/275°F/gas 1 and line two baking trays with baking paper.

In your OCD-clean bowl, whisk the egg whites good and hard until they're really stiff, so stiff that you could hold the bowl upside down over your head and they wouldn't fall out. Be very sure they are stiff enough before you attempt this manoeuvre. Add half of the sugar, continuing to whisk until the mix goes satiny, then add the rest of the sugar.

Using a cocktail stick, add a small amount of food colouring. Whisk, and if it's blue enough for you, stop. If you'd prefer it to be more blue, add a tiny bit more – only a tiny amount, a little goes a long way – and whisk again. When you've achieved the requisite blueness, use a tablespoon to dollop golf ball-sized rounds of meringue on to the baking trays.

Bake for 1 hour 20 minutes, then turn the oven off and let the meringues sit in there, overnight. (If you need the oven for something else, I'm sure you can take them out and leave them on the worktop. Either way, you must leave them overnight.)

The following day, just before serving, break the meringues up into bite-sized pieces. Place a layer of these blue shards in the bottom of four little bowls. (Use glass bowls for maximum impact, but if you're like me and don't have any glass bowls, you can use wine glasses instead.) Spoon in a layer of blueberries, then a layer of yoghurt, then another layer of meringue and keep going in this fashion until the bowls or glasses are full, then stop. To top everything off, sprinkle with blue glitter.

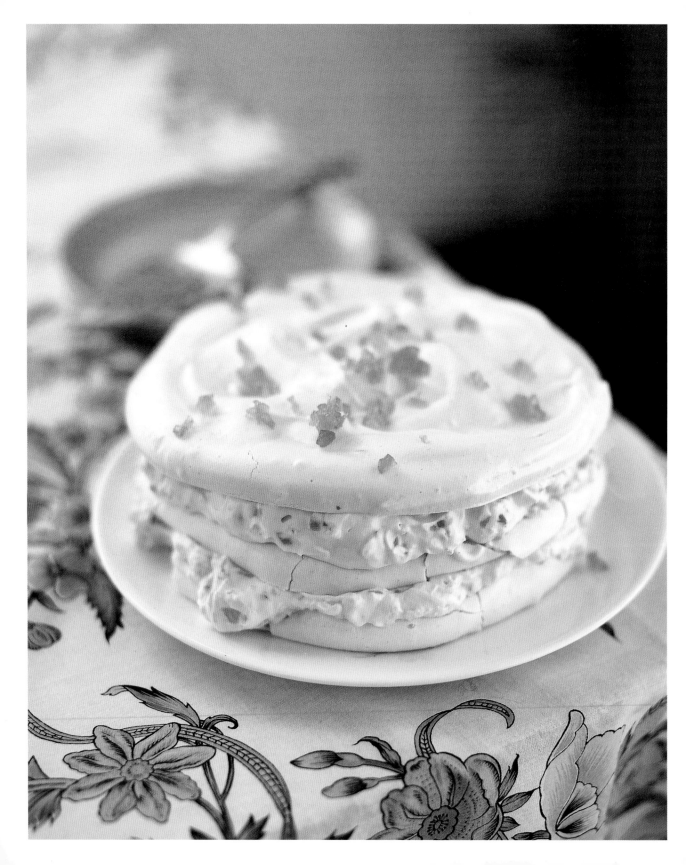

Shirley's Ginger and Pineapple Pavlova

Shirley is my very lovely mother-in-law and effortlessly produces all kinds of baking masterpieces with the minimum of fuss. This is an old favourite of Himself's – he goes misty-eyed whenever he talks about it. I've done my best here, but obviously it can never be as good as the one his mother makes.

Serves 6–8

For the meringue
3 egg whites
170g caster sugar

For the filling
6 pieces of stem ginger
250g fresh pineapple (or tinned will do, just drain off the juice from a 450g tin)
250ml double cream
1 tablespoon ginger syrup from the stem ginger

Preheat the oven to 80°C/150°F/gas ¼. Yes, this seems astonishingly low, but the baking goes on for a very long time, between 2½ and 3 hours. Line three baking trays with baking paper, then draw one circle on each sheet, 17cm in diameter. You can draw around the base of a cake tin, or the lid of a saucepan, whatever you have handy.

Whisk the egg whites until they're really stiff. Continuing to whisk, add a spoonful of sugar, then another. Keep at it until all the sugar is in. Divide the mixture equally – or as equally as you can – among the three baking trays, 'filling' the circles. Use your purple spatula (see page 16) to smooth the tops and edges.

Bake for at least 2½ hours, swapping the trays halfway through the cooking time, until the meringues are hard to the touch and have gone a very pale beige colour. If you'd like your cake to have a little bit of chew to it, take it out after 2½ hours, but if you'd prefer it more dry, go for the full 3 hours. Either way, whatever you decide, peel off the baking paper very carefully – these are fragile – and cool on the baking trays.

When they're fully cooled, chop the stem ginger very finely and the pineapple quite finely. Whisk the cream until it's holding its shape but not too stiff, then whip in the ginger syrup. Add the chopped ginger (reserving a sixth for decoration) and pineapple and stir through.

Place one meringue circle on a nice plate and cover it with half of the cream/ginger/pineapple mix. Place another meringue circle on top of this, then add the rest of the cream. Place – yes! You saw this coming! – your third piece of meringue on top. Neaten it up as best you can and sprinkle the top with the remaining chopped stem ginger. This is a delicious cake. But not as delicious as if Shirley herself had made it. Obviously.

Zagina Reforma Torta
(Zaga's Reform* Chocolate Cake)

Now, you already know who Zaga is from the honey cake recipe (see page 107) and, like I said, she's an amazing cook.

This is a fabulous cake, very special – Zaga used to make it for Ljiljana's birthdays. It's a meringue that is combined with a high quantity of ground nuts and this makes it quite 'cakey', even though there's no flour in it. What is really nice is that the leftover egg yolks are used to create an intensely rich chocolate icing. Usually I don't know what to do with the leftover yolks so I 'temporarily' put them in the Bowl of Shame (see page 21). This I put in the fridge, telling myself elaborate lies about all the things I'll make with the yolks – pastry, omelettes, whatever. But I don't and over the next 2 days, the guilt builds and builds until I can hardly go into the kitchen, then at some point I 'break', run in really fast and in a mad frenzy, empty the yolks into the bin.

Now, about this cake – it's done in four layers (my first! I'd never gone higher than three layers before!). The multilayeredness is the best thing about it because it's visually stunning, but it means you need four tins (17cm, if possible). I know most people won't have four tins, all the same size. Maybe you could borrow some? Or you could try baking the bases in two goes? Or, as Zaga says, 'One of the ideas is to bake the whole in the big baking tray that you get with the cooker and then cut it in four pieces.'

Serves 12–14

10 eggs

500g caster sugar

300g hazelnuts, ground to crumbs

150g dark chocolate (70% cocoa solids)

250g butter, at room temperature

*We couldn't get to the bottom of the name. Maybe it's because the eggs get split and then 'reform'?

Get a good night's sleep the night before. You need your wits about you for this cake.

Grease four 17cm tins, then line with baking paper. Preheat the oven to 180°C/350°F/gas 4.

Separate the eggs. Whisk the 10 egg whites and when they're firm, add 300g of the sugar, reserving the rest for the icing. Then add the ground hazelnuts, mix well, then pour into your tin (or tins) using your palette knife to smooth the top. Bake for 15 minutes. Turn out on to a wire rack – there might be a bit of a queue – and leave until fully cooled.

Now, for the icing. In a heavy saucepan, bring about 2 litres of water to the boil. Reduce down to a simmer, then put the bowl containing the 10 egg yolks over the water (but not in it). Add the remaining 200g of sugar, then whisk – so that you're heating and whisking simultaneously, if that makes sense. I'd never done this before, it was all new and wonderful. •••

As the yolks cook, their consistency will change and thicken. We're walking a fine line here because we don't want to scramble the eggs, but they do need to reach 160°C so that they're not raw eggs and so you don't run the risk of giving people – or indeed yourself – salmonella. You can check this by using a thermometer if you have one (I don't). Or else the mixture will coat a metal spoon or bubble at the edge of the bowl. I admit I was very anxious about this, but it was nice to have something real to be anxious about, instead of the usual random free-floating stuff.

When the yolks are hot enough, start dropping the chocolate in, chunk by chunk, so that it melts. Keep whisking. When all the chocolate is melted, take the bowl off the heat and leave to cool fully. Cream the butter and beat it well into the cooled yolky-chocolate mix.

Then it's time to assemble the cake and this is the bit I found the most challenging. Place a layer of cake on a plate – pick the biggest piece of cake, I know theoretically they're all the same size, but mine weren't – then spread on a thick layer of the icing. Carefully add the next layer of cake (the second biggest) on top of the icing, working hard to centre it so that its edges line up with the edges of the layer underneath. This required more skill than I had anticipated.

Spread on another thick layer of icing, then add the next layer of cake and so on until all four layers are stacked (neatly, hopefully) on top of each other, glued together with the lovely thick icing. Cover the top and sides of the cake with the rest of the icing and refrigerate for a couple of hours.

BUT! Watch it like a hawk! Check it every 15 minutes because it might start 'sliding' – some of the middle layers might break formation and start bulging like hernias. If this happens, encourage them – gently but firmly – back into place by poking with the flat side of your purple spatula (see page 16). Yes, it happened to me, there was some slippage, but it really didn't matter. People were amazed and astounded by this cake. My friends were in awe and my enemies were sickened.

Banana Meringue Pie

As with the previous recipe, *this* should only be attempted when you have lots of time and a great desire to concentrate on something other than yourself. This is a three-part challenge – you have to make and bake the pastry base (take a look at the Pastry section of this book if you haven't made pastry before), you have to create the banana custard from scratch and you have to whip, whirl and bake the meringue topping. Even cutting this beast into slices has to be done in a special way. However! Yes, however! The finished pie looks and tastes AMAZING. You will be so proud of yourself.

Serves 6–8

For the pastry
170g plain flour
pinch of salt
100g cold butter,
  cut into cubes

For the banana custard
500ml milk
130g caster sugar
100g plain flour
¼ teaspoon salt
4 egg yolks (keep the whites
  for the meringue later)
1 teaspoon banana essence*
55g butter, chilled and cut
  into cubes
4 medium bananas

For the meringue
4 egg whites
170g caster sugar
¼ teaspoon cream of tartar
pinch of salt

*I know I shouldn't be advocating artificial stuff, but I adore banana essence. I get it in my local Asian shop. It's so riddled with chemicals that I think it might actually be illegal. Nevertheless, delicious.

Make the pastry by sieving the flour and salt into a bowl, then adding the cubed butter. Use the tips of your fingers to rub small pieces of butter and small pieces of flour together, until the mix begins to resemble fine breadcrumbs. Add a tablespoon or two of cold water if needed.

Refrigerate the pastry for an hour, then roll it out on to a floured surface. Preheat the oven to 180°C/350°F/gas 4, and liberally butter a 20cm pie tin or dish with a 5cm depth and line it with the pastry.

Blind bake for 15 minutes, then remove from the oven and keep standing by.

To make the banana custard, start by scalding the milk (see page 21). In a separate saucepan – a big one, big enough to eventually hold all the custard ingredients – sieve the sugar, flour and salt. Gradually whisk in the hot milk. Stirring constantly – the mixture will go really quite thick and resistant, you should build up a bit of a sweat – bring to the boil, cook for 1 minute, then remove from the heat.

In a separate bowl, whisk the egg yolks for a couple of minutes, then slowly add in a cupful of the hot milk/sugar mix. Keep whisking until fully incorporated, then pour all of this egg yolk/flour/sugar mix into the saucepan, where the majority of the milk/sugar mix awaits you. (The reason for all this toing and froing is to even out the temperature, so that the egg yolks don't scramble.)

Cook over a low heat for a few minutes and the mixture will thicken up even more. Remove from the heat, then add the banana essence and the cubed butter. Stir until the butter has melted, then leave the mix to cool down to room temperature. Because this is a custard, there's a high likelihood that a skin will form on the surface. If the thought of this gives you the shudders, cover the custard with a circle of baking paper – like, literally have the baking paper resting on the custard, not just above it.

Slice the bananas thinly and line the pastry base with them, in an overlapping pattern. When the custard has cooled, remove the baking paper. Scoop the custard into the pastry case, covering the

•••

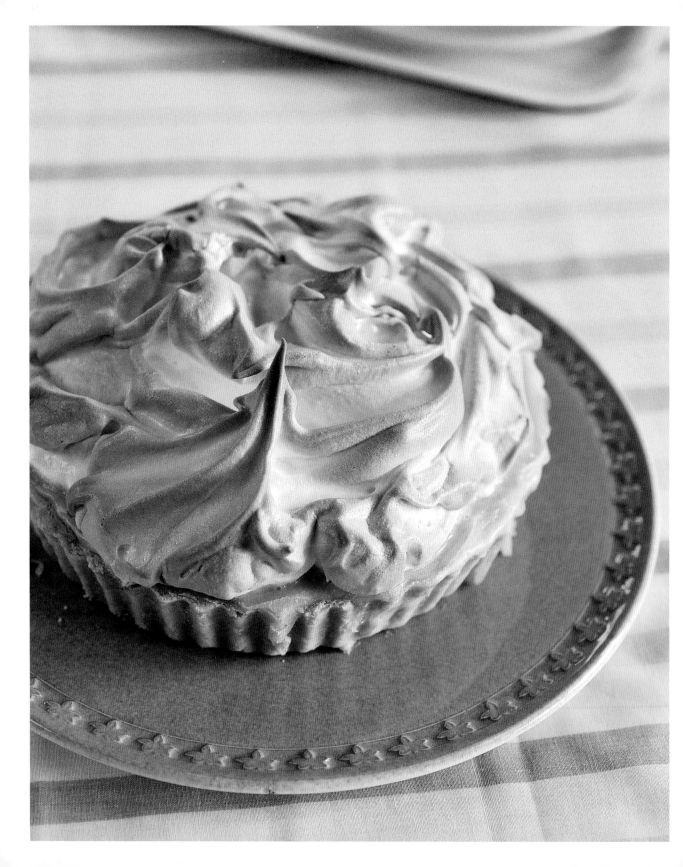

sliced bananas. Use your purple spatula (see page 16) to spread it evenly. Leave to set for a couple of hours.

When the time is upon you, preheat the oven to 180°C/350°F/gas 4.

Make the meringue by beating the egg whites until they're stiff. Gradually add the sugar, then the cream of tartar and salt. Swirl the meringue on top of the set custard, making sure it comes right to the edges of the pastry because when it bakes and eventually cools, it will contract slightly and you don't want it exposing the filling underneath.

Bake for 20 minutes, until it's a pale beige colour and crisp to the touch. However! WARNING! WARNING! WARNING! The eggs won't be cooked through, so don't give this otherwise impeccable pie to vulnerable types – by that, I mean children, old folk, pregnant women and people with compromised immune systems. It's very unlikely that they'll get salmonella, but like I said on page 108, we live in litigious times. Also, you don't want anything bad on your conscience – God knows, we struggle enough with existential guilt without having poisoned someone, no? Cool the pie on a rack, then refrigerate for a couple of hours.

To slice: SPECIAL INSTRUCTIONS! Have a bowl of very hot water standing by. Dip a sharp knife into the hot water, and cut a slice through the meringue, but not down into the custard and pastry. Dip the knife into the water again, then do another slice through the meringue. Continue to mark out slices through the meringue, re-dipping the knife in the water after each go. When all the slices are marked out in the meringue, then, and only then, cut all the way down through the custard and pastry. Serve cold.

You can do this; you CAN make **MACAROONS**. However, they will not be all lovely and neat and the same size, the way they are in Ladurée. Can you make your peace with that? If not, stop right here, you'll only wreck your head. But if you can accept that your macaroons may be bockety and funny-shaped and still worthy of existence, then proceed.

To get the same consistency every time, professional bakers weigh their egg whites, allowing only a certain amount into the bowl. However, we are not professional bakers. We take our chances, we live on the edge, we accept that some egg whites are bigger than others and therefore every batch of macaroons we make will be unique. We do not despair over this, oh no, we celebrate their individuality.

Basic Cranberry Macaroons

This is a 'flavourless' macaroon – the flavouring comes from the filling – so you can use this recipe to make countless varieties. However, I do like to colour each batch to match its flavour. I use edible gel rather than a liquid colouring because the liquid can cause the meringue to 'collapse' and flow all over the baking tray and, God knows, as dispiriting experiences go, that's a bad one.

Makes approx. 30 'single' macaroons, which means 15 pairs

For the macaroons
2 egg whites
150g caster sugar
120g ground almonds
120g icing sugar
pink food colouring,
 the gel type

For the filling
150ml whipping cream
2 tablespoons cranberry
 sauce*

*Yes, like you have with your turkey at Christmas, it's basically jam.

Don't turn the oven on yet. Line two baking trays with baking paper. Using a round 4cm cookie cutter and a soft pencil, draw twelve circles on the baking paper, leaving a good 5cm between each circle. (You don't HAVE to do this, it's just that I found it useful to know roughly how much mix I should be putting out for each macaroon.) Then turn the paper over, so that the pencilled side is facing downward, because otherwise the pencil marks will come off on the macaroons and you'll end up eating them. I don't think pencils are poisonous, but let's not take any chances and you'll still be able to see the marked circles, so it's all okay. Try to make sure that the baking paper is totally flat (use Sellotape if you have to), because the macaroons are so light that if there's even a slight slope in the paper, they will take on that shape. Do your 'level' best. (Pun.)

Whisk the egg whites until they're stiff. Add a tablespoon of the caster sugar and whisk again. Keep adding the sugar and keep whisking. When it's all in, add in the ground almonds, the icing sugar and your coloured gel. Mix thoroughly.

Right. Can you face a piping bag? If not, don't worry. Just use two teaspoons to fill in the little circles on the baking paper with the mixture. 'Encourage' them into neat circle shapes but DON'T GO MAD. If we're going down the piping bag route, I salute you. Here we go. Put a 1cm plain nozzle into your piping bag and fold back a 5cm 'cuff' on the bag. I'm sorry if this is horribly baffling. If you feel like crying, just use the teaspoon method instead, I beg you. Don't make yourself miserable. But if you're looking for distraction, let's carry on. Pile the mix into the bag and push it down towards the bottom, trying to get air bubbles out. When it's all in, unroll the 'cuff' and twist the bag closed. •••

Holding the piping bag directly above the centre of one of the circles on the baking tray, squeeze out a macaroon by twisting the piping bag. When the circle is full, whip off the bag with a flourish, leaving your macaroon behind. There will be a big, mad, pointy head on it. Don't worry, it will subside in the oven. Now repeat the exercise again. Keep at it. Keep going, and when you've emptied the piping bag, take a moment to congratulate yourself. Leave the trays to stand on the worktop for about half an hour – this gives the macaroons a nice crusty outside.

Preheat the oven to 150°C/300°F/gas 2, then bake for 25 minutes. Cool on a wire rack, then after 20 minutes, use your palette knife to lift the macaroons off the baking paper. Be gentle because they're fragile. Pretend you're dealing with yourself.

Leave them to cool a while longer and in the meantime make your filling. Whip the cream until it holds its shape, then stir in the cranberry sauce. Use the cream mixture to sandwich the macaroons together in pairs, 'matching' them by putting small ones with small ones, oval ones with oval ones and so on. Also – only if you'd like – putting any cracked or deformed ones into the bottom layers. Finally, admire them. Celebrate their unique bocketyness. Then celebrate your own.

Mango Macaroons

Exactly the same as the Basic Cranberry Macaroons except I used yellow food colouring (Squires' Daffodil, not quite yellow enough for my liking, but we live and learn) instead of pink and used mango jam instead of cranberry sauce.

Apple Macaroons

Exactly the same as the Basic Cranberry Macaroons except I used green food colouring (a half-and-half mix of Sugarflair's Gooseberry and Christmas Green to be exact) and used apple spread instead of cranberry sauce.

Bluegrass Macaroons

Exactly the same as the Basic Cranberry Macaroons except I used Squires' Bluegrass food colouring instead of pink and didn't use any flavouring with the cream because I don't know what 'Bluegrass' tastes like and frankly, with a colour this fabulous (very similar to Tiffany blue), who cares if it tastes of nothing?

And so on . . . using an infinite variety of colourings and flavours. The pleasure of it.

Tiramisu Macaroons

We're stepping things up a notch here, but don't be alarmed. What makes these 'tiramisu' macaroons as opposed to any other kind, is the filling. The macaroons themselves are almost identical to the Basic Cranberry Macaroons.

Makes 15 pairs

For the macaroons

2 egg whites

150g golden caster sugar

120g ground almonds

120g icing sugar

1 tablespoon instant coffee, dissolved in a tablespoon of boiling water, then fully cooled

cocoa powder, for dusting

For the filling

100g mascarpone cheese

1 tablespoon Marsala wine (optional)*

1 tablespoon instant coffee, dissolved in a tablespoon of boiling water, then cooled

*The alcohol will not be cooked off, so don't give this to children or people who need to avoid alcohol.

Line two baking trays with baking paper, using the instructions in the Basic Cranberry Macaroons (see page 151).

Whisk the egg whites until stiff, gradually add the caster sugar, then the almonds and icing sugar, the usual blah. Where you want to pay attention is when you add the coffee. When I say 'dissolved in a tablespoon of boiling water', I mean that literally. Just a tablespoon. On my first few attempts to make these, I used too much liquid and the uncooked macaroons just flowed all over the baking tray and ran into each other into one big, flat disaster. Also, the coffee must be fully cooled, because if it's not, the heat will affect the consistency of the meringue, again making it madly runny. So, add your 1 tablespoon of cooled, dissolved coffee and stir carefully.

Using either two teaspoons or a piping bag (see page 151), create your macaroons on your baking paper. Leave to stand for about half an hour, then heat the oven to 140°C/275°F/gas 1.

Bake for 30 minutes, then cool on wire racks. Use a palette knife to lift the macaroons off the baking paper and when they're fully cooled, make the filling by beating the mascarpone until smooth, then mixing together gradually with the Marsala and dissolved coffee. If it goes very runny – by that I mean so runny that it will just run off the sides of the macaroons – put it into the fridge for a while. When it has re-firmed to your satisfaction, use it to sandwich the macaroons into pairs. Finally, sprinkle over a light dusting of cocoa powder through a sieve.

Very Chocolatey Macaroons

What makes these slightly different from my other macaroon recipes is that I'm using melted chocolate and this affects the consistency. It 'collapses' the meringue, knocking the air out of it, so there's no need for any fiddling with piping bags here. No point. The mix will be too runny.

The finish on these boyos will be rougher and more rustic looking, less smooth and sophisticated. Don't be alarmed. You've done nothing wrong. Also, these macaroons are bigger than the other ones, which can only be good.

Makes approx. 12 pairs

For the macaroons

100g dark chocolate
(70% cocoa solids)

3 egg whites

150g caster sugar

150g ground almonds

1 tablespoon cocoa powder,
seived

For the buttercream filling

225g butter

50g cocoa powder

300g icing sugar

2 tablespoons milk

1 teaspoon vanilla extract

Preheat the oven to 140°C/275°F/gas 1. Line two baking trays with baking paper, but there's no need to draw any little circles.

Melt the chocolate using your chosen method (see page 20), then set aside to cool.

Whip the egg whites until stiff. Gradually add the sugar, continuing to beat. Stir in the almonds, the sieved cocoa powder, then the melted chocolate. The meringue will now collapse (i.e. all the air will go out of it and it will seem a lot smaller). Hold your nerve.

Scoop heaped tablespoons of the mix on to the baking trays and bake for an hour. Cool on a wire rack for 20 minutes, then use your palette knife to lift the macaroons off the baking paper.

Make the buttercream by beating the butter until light and fluffy. Slowly add the cocoa and icing sugar. When fully incorporated, add the milk and vanilla and beat to a spreading consistency. Use this chocolate buttercream to sandwich the macaroons into pairs.

BISCUITS AND COOKIES

Orange and Fennel Tuiles

Chocolate and Treacle Biscuits

Breakfast Bars

Shakar Loqum (Armenian Sugar Cookies)

Lebkuchen Hearts

Pistachio Biscotti

Defibrillator Cubes

Luxury Blueberry, Pine Nut and Chocolate Cookies

Shoe and Handbag Biscuits

There's such a massive universe of **BISCUITS AND COOKIES** out there for our delectation that at times it really does make me believe in a benign God. Never mind butterflies; never mind a newborn baby's foot. For me it's all about the biscuits! God created a world where biscuits exist! When you look at it like that, how could She be anything but a decent sort!

Obviously, you'd need to write an entire encyclopedia to cover the multitude of biscuits and cookies in the world and all I have available is a chapter. So I've made a pitiful attempt (the nerve of me, the neck of me, the grandiosity of me) to give the merest glimpse of what's available to us. I've started with thin and sophisticated tuiles, made my way to rustic oaty bruisers and done some detours en route.

I must admit to you that of all the things I've ever baked, making biscuits has given me the most pleasure. Because it's where I get to use my (many, many) cookie cutters and really, I cannot tell you! I get to make shoes. Edible shoes. And handbags. And owls. And stars. And hearts. If I found out I had an hour left to live, I'd use the time to make shoe biscuits. Fact.

Orange and Fennel Tuiles

These are very much 'lady' biscuits. Like, you wouldn't serve them to the man who's come to fix your washing machine. Not unless you wanted him to stalk out in disgust. Nevertheless, in their thin, delicate, melt-in-the-mouth way, these are fabulous – sort of like orange-and-fennel-flavoured air.

One important thing to note, though, is that it seems to be the 'done thing' to 'shape' one's tuiles so that they're curved. From what I can gather, flatness in a tuile is not considered to be a good look.

The best way to curve them is, *the very second* they come out of the oven, to lay them on a rolling pin or wine bottle and press gently. They'll take on the shape of the pin or bottle but won't break. However, please be aware that they're pliable only for *a very short time*. I mean, literally seconds. Perhaps 30. I've discovered the hard way that the best way to do this is to remove maybe three or four tuiles from the oven, lay them on whatever curved thing you're using, let them cool, move them on to a plate, then take three or four more tuiles out of the oven and start again. The good thing is that they cool and set really quickly, so at least you won't have to do too much hanging around.

Makes approx. 15

50g butter
½ teaspoon fennel seeds
2 egg whites
110g icing sugar
50g plain flour
zest of 1 orange

Line two large baking trays with baking paper and preheat your oven to 180°C/350°F/gas 4.

Melt the butter and set aside until fully cooled.

Grind the fennel seeds well to release their flavour.

Whip the egg whites until they hold soft peaks.

Sieve in the icing sugar and flour, then add the orange zest, fennel seeds and the melted, cooled butter. Fold through with as light a touch as you can manage.

For each tuile, pour a level soup spoon of the mix, which will be quite runny, on to the baking paper and leave room – a good 3cm between each – for spreading. Keep going until you've used up all the mix. The tuiles will look very insubstantial, almost see-through. Don't worry, they're meant to.

Bake for between 6 and 12 minutes, until the tuiles are golden around the edges but still pale in the middle. Use your palette knife to gently remove them from the baking paper. If you're planning on 'shaping' them, now's your time.

Serve to people who don't really believe in eating.

Chocolate and Treacle Biscuits

Dark, rich, sophisticated chocolate biscuits. The treacle adds an extra depth of flavour.

Makes about 18 biscuits

150g dark chocolate
 (70% cocoa solids)
100g butter
150g light muscovado sugar
1 egg
1 tablespoon black treacle
110g plain flour
30g cocoa powder
pinch of salt

Line two big baking trays with baking paper.

Melt the chocolate using your preferred method (see page 20) and let it cool for 10 to 15 minutes.

Then – and only then – preheat the oven to 180°C/350°F/gas 4.

Beat the butter and sugar until pale and fluffy.

Add in the egg and treacle and mix well.

Add the (cooled) melted chocolate and keep mixing.

Sieve in the flour, the cocoa powder and the pinch of salt and fold through.

Using two soup spoons, scoop up golf ball-sized lumps of the dough (it will be very sticky) and place on the baking paper.

Keep plenty of space between them – they will spread.

Bake for 15 minutes, but check on them after about 12 because these have a tendency to burn.

Cool the trays on wire racks. The biscuits will still be quite soft at this stage so don't be 'at' them. After perhaps half an hour, gently remove them from their trays, but keep them cooling on the racks. After a while the outsides of the biscuits will crisp up and the insides will be wonderfully melty and chocolatey.

Breakfast Bars

This almost qualifies as healthy eating. I started making these when myself and a group of friends decided we needed a hobby and fixed on hill walking in Wicklow. The nuts, seeds and dried fruit give me the energy to go for the final push when I'm trudging up the side of a mountain, and the condensed milk gives a bit of sweet comfort when the sleet is blowing in my face, I feel like crying and I wish I'd picked a different hobby, maybe doing stained glass.

Makes 14

200ml condensed milk

150g porridge oats

100g dried apricots

60g crystallized ginger

100g hazelnuts

60g pumpkin seeds

30g sunflower seeds

1 tablespoon cocoa powder (optional)*

*In fact, it's so optional that it doesn't exist on my official list of ingredients. I prefer to lie about its presence because people feel so virtuous eating these delicious bars that I'd feel bad about wrecking their buzz.

Preheat the oven to 130°C/250°F/gas 1. Line a 20cm square tin with baking paper.

Gently heat the condensed milk in a saucepan.

Put the porridge oats in a separate bowl.

Chop the apricots and ginger and halve the hazelnuts, then add to the porridge oats, along with the pumpkin and sunflower seeds.

Pour in the condensed milk and stir well. The mix will go lovely and sticky.

Add the sneaky tablespoon of cocoa powder, then wipe the whole episode from your mind.

Pile the mix into the tin and pack down well, getting into all the corners. Flatten the surface using the back of a tablespoon dipped in water.

Bake for an hour.

Cool on a wire tray, then remove from the tin and cut into bar shapes, roughly 10cm by 3cm.

Climb the side of a hill, then eat without guilt.

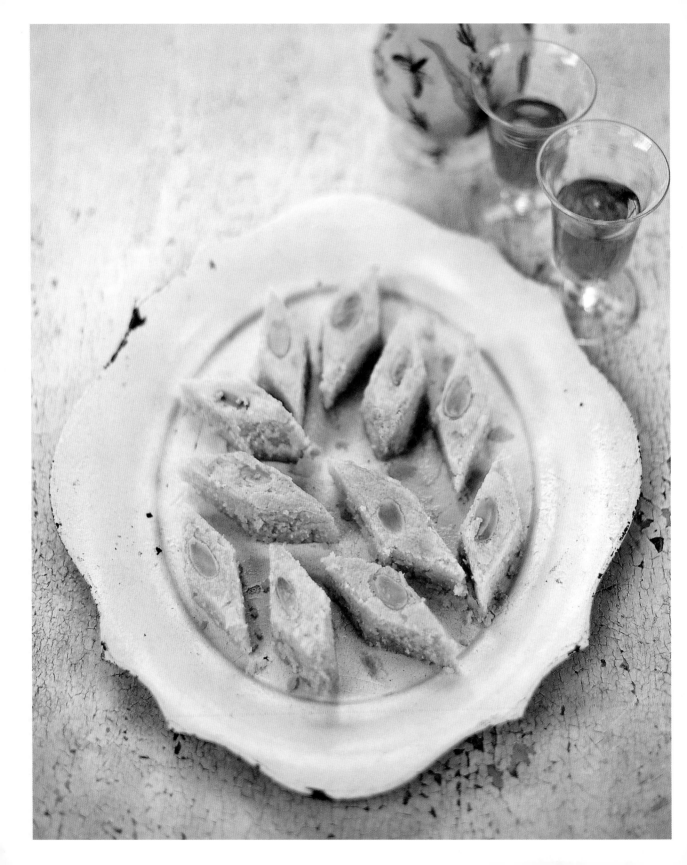

Shakar Loqum (Armenian Sugar Cookies)

This is an amazing recipe from my brother-in-law, Sean, who is an absolute genius in the kitchen. His mother JoAnn was of Armenian descent and Sean sent me this recipe, entitled, 'From my Mom's recipe box'. I found this almost unbearably poignant, as JoAnn died way too young. But maybe it's of some comfort to know that so many of us are enjoying the sugar cookies she used to make.

These diamond-shaped cookies are intense – buttery, sweet and slightly crumbly. Don't be alarmed by how small they are – they are so very, very rich that to make them any bigger would lessen their impact. Also, they might trigger a cardiac arrest.

Makes about 22 cookies

335g clarified butter – also known as ghee*

170g caster sugar

pinch of salt

pinch of baking powder

2 eggs, separated

375g plain flour

approximately 30 slivered almonds

* You can get clarified butter in Asian shops. Or you can make your own, but it's pretty labour intensive. Also, I find the idea of doing it terribly frightening, but you mightn't. Here are JoAnn's instructions:

Melt about 420g butter over a low heat until foam appears. Skim off the foam using a knife and keep on the low heat for about 15 minutes. During this time, water will evaporate and salts and solids will settle at the bottom of the pan. Cool for about 15 to 20 minutes, then carefully pour the clarified butter into a container, leaving the salts and solids at the bottom of the pan. You can discard these.

Grease and line a 20cm loose-bottomed square tin and preheat the oven to 180°C/350°F/gas 4.

Whisk the clarified butter, then add the sugar, salt and baking powder and mix well. Add the egg yolks and mix again. Sieve in the flour, stir it through with a wooden spoon, then use your hands to shape the dough. Press the dough into the prepared tin and flatten it with the base of a glass.

Now, things get a little tricky. The authentic way to make Shakar Loqum is to cut the uncooked dough into diamond shapes, and it was the part of the recipe I found most challenging. You might find it helpful (I did) to do a dry run first by getting a sheet of paper, the same size as the baking tin, and drawing the diamond patterns, so that you know what you want to recreate on the dough. (To be quite honest, I got Himself to do it. He's good that way, patient and mathematical.)

Draw diagonal lines, approximately 2.5cm apart, going in one direction, then draw diagonal lines going in the opposite direction, also about 2.5cm apart. Remember that you want diamond shapes, not squares, so the lines should be at a fairly acute angle. You want long, narrow biscuits, not short, squat ones. Am I making any sense to you at all? If not, I'm so sorry. Just look at the picture if you're confused.

Now recreate your drawing by using a small sharp knife to cut the uncooked dough into diamond shapes, the same size and shape as the ones in your drawing. You can now discard your piece of paper.

Place a slice of almond into the middle of each diamond shape. Beat the egg whites lightly, then brush the top of the dough with them. (You won't get to use all the egg whites.)

Bake for 15 minutes, then reduce the oven heat to 150°C/300°F/gas 2 and bake for about another 20 minutes, until the biscuits are a golden brown colour.

Remove the tin from the oven and while the biscuits are still warm (and still in the tin), recut the diamond shapes – by that I mean go

•••

over the pre-existing 'cuts' with the same small sharp knife, so that the biscuits will fully separate into diamond shapes when they're eventually removed from the tin. It may not be immediately obvious where the diagonal lines are, but actually the almond slivers worked as great reference points.

Wait until they're fully cold before carefully removing the cookies from the tin.

There will be a few leftover bits of biscuit at the sides of the tin that didn't make it into the diamond shapes. This might initially strike you as wastage, but then remind yourself of what Confucius once said (at least I think it was him.) 'Broken Biscuits Don't Count.' Eat them without guilt.

Thanks, JoAnn. (And thanks, Sean.)

Lebkuchen Hearts

The first time I encountered these delicious spicy German cookies was one Christmas several years ago when my German publisher sent me a massive one (about 20cm in diameter) with *Ich Liebe Dich* iced on it (which means, 'I Love You'.) I was thrilled and all set to tuck into it until Himself suggested that the fact it was hanging off a ribbon meant that it was probably intended to be a Christmas decoration, rather than a Christmas sweetmeat. This, of course, came as a terrible disappointment to me.

So I investigated the whole Lebkuchen hearts business and discovered that yes, there is a German tradition of giving them as home decorations. Or sometimes the recipient wears them on a ribbon around their neck (I think that's *gorgeous*.) And it seems to be the done thing to ice cute sayings on them.

But the point I'm trying to make is that these biscuits *can* be eaten. In fact, they *should* be eaten because they taste fabulous.

Don't be alarmed by the long list of spices in the recipe. I think the most important one is ginger and if you don't have any of the others, don't fret.

Finally, as these are Lebkuchen *hearts*, you'll need some sort of heart-shaped cookie cutter. If you don't have any, you could try freestyling with a sharp knife. Or you could simply use a different-shaped cutter and change the name of the cookies to – oh, just off the top of my head – Lebkuchen Shoes. Or Lebkuchen Handbags. •••

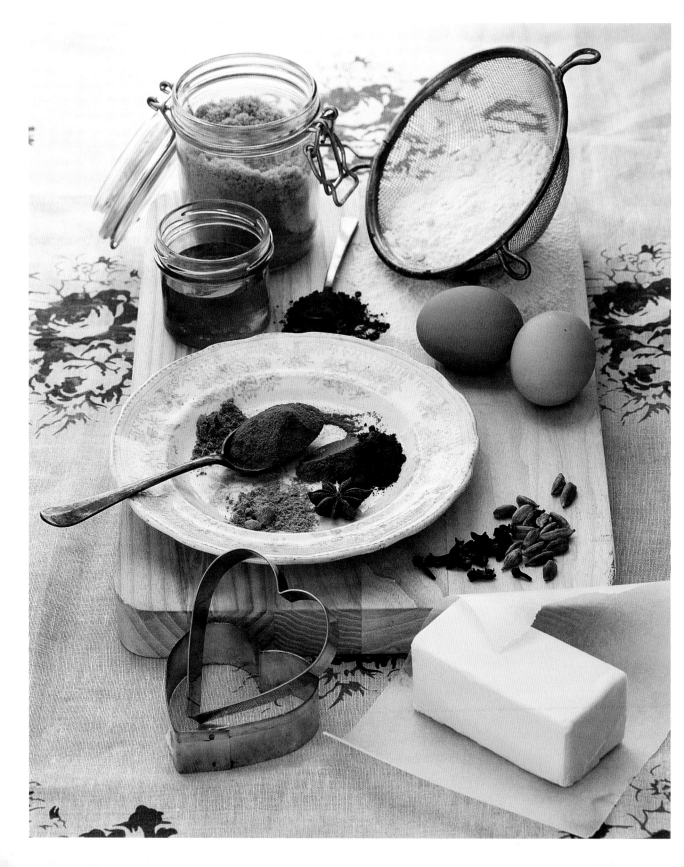

Makes approx.

18 heart-shaped cookies
(10cm at their widest point)
or 3 giant ones (25cm at
their widest point)

100g butter

275g honey

100g light brown soft sugar

1 teaspoon ground ginger

1 teaspoon ground coriander

1 teaspoon ground cinnamon

1 teaspoon ground allspice

½ teaspoon ground nutmeg

2 cloves, bashed

1 star of anise

6 cardamom pods, bashed

2½ tablespoons cocoa
powder

600g plain flour

pinch of salt

1½ teaspoons baking powder

1 egg

To decorate
writing icing*

*I used Dr. Oetker's for the
fine lines and Wilton's for
the fatter stuff.

If you want to keep things
authentically German, here
are a few handy phrases:

Ich liebe dich
(I love you)

Ich liebe schuhe
(I love shoes)

Fröhliche Weihnachten
(Happy Christmas)

Place the butter, honey, sugar, spices and cocoa powder in a medium-sized saucepan and heat gently. Stir until the sugar dissolves and the whole mix looks dark and treacly. Be careful not to let it burn. Take off the heat and cool slightly, and remove the cardamom, star anise and cloves.

Sieve the flour with the salt and baking powder into a bowl. Using your fist, make a crater in the flour and add the egg, then pour in the honey mixture. Mix on a low speed and eventually a ball of dough will form.

Divide it roughly into two, wrap each lump in clingfilm and stick in the fridge for at least a couple of hours (you could leave it as long as a couple of days).

When you're ready to make your hearts, line two baking trays with baking paper and heat the oven to 180°C/350°F/gas 4.

Scatter your work surface with flour and roll out one of your lumps of dough until it's about 1.5cm thick. These are quite hefty creatures, so no need to roll them out too thin.

If you're going for the 10cm heart-shaped cookies, press the cutter right down into the rolled-out dough until it reaches the floured surface, then give it a tiny little 'shimmy' to loosen it. Gently manoeuvre your palette knife under the raw cookie and lift on to the baking tray. If it all goes a bit gammy, and it might well, especially if you're new to this game, just roll out the dough and try again. (The experts say you shouldn't roll out dough more than once, that it makes it slightly tough, but it's all very well for them, after all, they're *experts*.)

Remember if you want to make hearts that will hang from a ribbon, create a little hole for the ribbon to go through.

To make a giant heart, as I say, you can freestyle or if you're lucky enough (as I am) to have a heart-shaped tin, press it down on to the dough and cut around it. That bit went okay. It was when I tried to transfer the heart on to the baking tray that it went awry on me and broke in half (metaphor, inadvertent, but clearly no escaping it). However, I pieced it back together and although you could still see the join, it was grand. (Another metaphor, obviously.)

Roll out your second lump of dough and repeat the process.

Bake for 15 to 20 minutes, watching that they don't catch on the bottom. Obviously the bigger the cookie, the longer it will take.

Let the cookies cool completely on their tray. They will harden as they cool.

You can serve these plain – they are really delicious, dark and spicy and very Christmassy. Or you can decorate with writing icing.

Pistachio Biscotti

Home-made biscotti! The thrill! Who knew such things were possible? This recipe calls for a tablespoon of nut oil and I've suggested using pistachio oil because once upon a time, by bizarre chance, I found a tin of it (not even a jar! A tin!) gathering dust at the back of a shelf in a faraway deli and have been looking for a chance to use it ever since. I'd never seen such a thing as pistachio oil before, or since, and the likelihood of you being able to lay your hands on some might be slim. In which case, use olive oil instead and don't give it a moment's worry.

Makes 12–14 biscotti

120g plain flour

½ teaspoon baking powder

3 teaspoons cocoa powder

75g caster sugar

25g butter, chilled and cut into cubes

1 egg

1 tablespoon pistachio oil*

40g pistachios, halved

50g dark chocolate (70% cocoa solids), chopped roughly

*Or if, as it almost certainly will, it proves impossible to find, olive oil will do instead.

Line a baking tray with greaseproof paper and preheat the oven to 160°C/325°F/gas 3.

Sieve the flour, baking powder and cocoa powder into a bowl, then stir in the sugar.

Add the butter and either rub in with your fingertips or blitz with your machine until the butter has all 'disappeared.' The mix will look like dark sand.

Beat the egg and the oil together, then add to the flour/cocoa, etc. and mix well. At this stage it should start coming together to form a dough.

Add the pistachios and chopped chocolate and stir to distribute evenly.

Sprinkle your worktop with flour. Divide the dough into two and, using your hands, roll it out into two logs, each about 25cm long. Slightly flatten the logs until they are 4cm to 5cm wide.

Bake for 20 minutes. Remove from the oven and lower the temperature to 150°C/300°F/gas 2.

Using a serrated knife, slice each log into six or seven evenly sized pieces. Gently, because at this stage they're soft and fragile, put some space between each biscotto (singular of biscotti, I'm guessing!) then return to the oven for 10 minutes to dry out.

Remove from the oven and leave in the air to firm up and harden for a couple of hours.

Defibrillator Cubes

So called because these peanut, honey and banana squares are so tightly packed full of dense energy they could probably bring a person back from the dead. They're similar to the Breakfast Bars on page 164 in that they're both oat-based, but these are the turbo-charged versions.

Makes 16 squares

125g butter
125g crunchy peanut butter
150g light muscovado sugar
75g honey
150g porridge oats
100g dried bananas,
  chopped finely
50g roasted salted peanuts

Grease and line a 20cm square tin. Preheat the oven to 160°C/325°F/gas 3.

Put the butter, peanut butter, sugar and honey into a BIG saucepan (big enough to eventually fit the porridge oats and other ingredients). Gently heat until all the butters melt and the sugar dissolves.

Stir in the porridge oats, chopped dried banana and peanuts and distribute evenly.

Pour into the prepared tin, getting the mix into all the corners. Flatten with the back of a wet tablespoon and bake for 30 minutes.

Cool on a baking tray and leave for a long time, preferably overnight, before removing from the tin and cutting into squares. They will be sticky, caramelly and utterly delicious and don't be worried that they might look small because, believe me, a little goes a long, long way.

Luxury Blueberry, Pine Nut and Chocolate Cookies

I have a tendency to overdo everything and these yummy cookies are packed tight with 'stuff' – blueberries, pine nuts and chocolate chips. If you'd prefer your ratio of cookie dough to 'bits' to be a little less decadent, then just reduce the amount of berries, nuts and choc chips you add. In fact, you can reduce the quantities by half and you'll still get fabulous cookies. Also, bear in mind, you can add any version of dried fruit and nuts. But try to make sure they're 'harmonious' – what I mean is that, for example, here, the sourness of the blueberries goes very well with the slight bitterness of the dark chocolate. And my one other tip is that whatever fruits and nuts you add, try to make sure that they're roughly the same size – in these cookies, the blueberries are roughly the same size as the pine nuts. What you don't want is *imbalance*.

These cookies include porridge oats, so they have a slightly rustic texture. But they taste so great that they'd be good enough to serve should anyone important ever be visiting you. Like, if George Michael just happened to drop in (God, how I wish . . .)

Makes approximately 18–20 cookies

125g butter
110g light brown soft sugar
65g dark brown soft sugar
1 egg
130g plain flour
30g cocoa powder
pinch of salt
½ teaspoon baking powder
70g porridge oats
100g dried blueberries
100g pine nuts
100g dark chocolate chips
   (70% cocoa solids)

Line two large baking trays with baking paper. Preheat the oven to 180°C/350°F/gas 4.

Beat the butter and sugars well together. Add the egg and beat again.

Sieve in the flour, cocoa powder, salt and baking powder and fold through.

Stir in the oats, blueberries, pine nuts and chocolate chips, distributing them evenly throughout. You might want to add the berries, nuts and chocolate chips in batches, so that if at some stage you feel the mix looks full enough, you can stop.

Using a soup spoon, scoop up rounds of the dough, roughly about the size of a golf ball, and use your hands to roll into a fairly flattened ball shape – your hands will get good and sticky but what harm – then place on the baking tray.

Leave plenty of space between each cookie because they'll spread as they cook.

Bake for 15 minutes, then cool the tray on a wire rack. Don't interfere with the cookies until they're fully cold because they'll be soft.

Then they'll be absolutely delicious – crunchy on the outside and melty and wonderful on the inside and – of course – jam-packed with bits and pieces.

Shoe and Handbag Biscuits

You don't only have to make shoe and handbag biscuits with this recipe. You can make *anything*. Anything! Your only limitation is your imagination. Also, the cookie cutters you have.

The flavouring I've used here is plain vanilla, but you can substitute any number of things – a teaspoon of dried cinnamon, the zest of half a lemon or a splash of Cointreau. For example, I've made cardamom and rosewater biscuits by adding four ground cardamom pods and a teaspoon of rosewater instead of the vanilla. I've also made lime and ginger biscuits by leaving out the vanilla and adding a teaspoon each of dried ginger and lime zest. It's up to you. Have fun. Go mad.

The same with the decorating. I've given you a basic glacé icing recipe, but you can dye it countless different colours and use writing icing, glitter, edible stars, sugar balls and so on to create any number of effects. There are plenty of websites that specialize in edible cake decorations and you will be introduced to a veritable wonderland. But a word of warning – once you start, you can't stop. You'll find yourself thinking, but I simply MUST have some of these tiny sugar cats! How can I make biscuits and hold my head up in polite society if they're not sprinkled with tiny sugar cats? Or mini candy canes! Or miniature edible butterflies!

If you're in any way prone to addiction, you could be in choppy waters here.

Makes a variable number depending on the size and shape of your cutters!

For the biscuits
200g butter
200g caster sugar
1 vanilla pod
1 egg, beaten
400g plain flour

For the icing
500g icing sugar
your choice of icing colour, writing icing and edible decorations

Beat the butter and sugar together until light and fluffy.

Scrape the vanilla seeds from the pod and add to the mix. Discard the pod.

Beat in the egg and sieve in the flour. Mix until a soft dough forms.

Divide the dough into two roughly equal-sized balls, cover with clingfilm and refrigerate for at least an hour.

Line three baking trays with baking paper. Preheat the oven to 180°C/350°F/gas 4.

Take the balls of pastry out of the fridge, remove the clingfilm and divide each one into two.

Roll one of the lumps out on a well-floured surface to a thickness of about 5mm. This is something you'll get better at gauging the more you do it, but there are some tools you can get in the specialist baking shops, such as special rubber bands to put on both ends of your rolling pin that limit the thickness of whatever you're rolling out, or 'guide sticks' – pieces of wood 5mm thick – that you place on either side of the pastry so you don't roll anything thinner. **•••**

Use the cookie cutter of your choice to cut out shapes. Press the cutter right down until it reaches the floured surface, then give it a tiny little 'shimmy' to loosen the shape from the pastry around it. Gently manoeuvre your palette knife under it and lift on to the baking paper. If it all goes a bit wrong, and it might well, especially if you're a beginner, then just roll out the pastry and try again.

You only need to leave a couple of centimetres between each biscuit on the tray because they don't spread much.

Gather up the scraps of unused pastry, roll them into your next ball of pastry and repeat until all your pastry is in biscuit shapes.

Bake for 9 to 12 minutes until the biscuits are a – funny, this – *biscuit* colour and are set but not too hard.

Take the trays from the oven and use your palette knife to lift each biscuit on to a wire rack. Cool.

Now for the icing. Use a wide-bottomed shallow bowl (that's assuming you have one and if you don't, don't worry, any bowl will do). Mix the icing sugar with 4 tablespoons cold water and your desired colouring until you have the runniness you desire.

Place a biscuit, face-side-down, in the bowl of icing until one surface is entirely covered. Tilt it from side to side, letting the excess icing run off (this is a messy business), then place on a wire rack. Even more icing might run off then. All fine. (You could place paper towels under the trays if you're worried about the mess.) Do a batch of perhaps eight biscuits, then decorate them before the icing has the chance to set. I use writing icing to define the edges and give a more 'finished' look, but that's entirely up to you. Either way, I predict you'll have a wonderful, wonderful, wonderful time. You'll feel like a child again.

FRUIT AND VEG

Beetroot Cake

Orange and Cashew Cake

Sweet Potato Pie

Chocolate Squash Tray Bake

Tamarind, Date and Sour Cherry Muffins

Mango Upside-Down Cake

Raspberry and Strawberry Upside-Down Cake

Pear, Almond and Tahini Cake

German Stollen Cake

Sweetcorn, Coconut and Lime Loaf

The healthy section!
A great way to get
your 5 a day. Er . . . yes.

Beetroot Cake

When I was young, I couldn't imagine anything more horrible than beetroot. I mean, *beetroot*. It was a strange, disgusting red ball that my father used to have with his salad and I was so horrified by it that whenever the jar appeared, I had to leave the house. Now I am older and less extreme in my opinions, I have tasted the fruit of the beetroot tree and I know it to be delicious.

Nevertheless, a funny choice for a cake, no? Well, no. Not when you think of carrot cake. After all, that's a root vegetable that has been successfully turned into cake. So why not beetroot? Well, when you put it like that . . .

It was hard though, hard to stop thinking of beetroot as a dinner ingredient and to start thinking of it as something that could coexist with sugar. I had to expend a lot of energy in a radical recalibration of my mental sweet/savoury interface. So much so that I couldn't summon the requisite will to grate raw beetroot. Yes, I decided to take the easy option and use beetroot that was already cooked. I urge you to do the same – raw beetroot is the hardest substance known to man. Also the reddest. It would take a day and a half to grate enough raw beetroot for this cake and your entire street would be dyed vermilion for ever.

Makes about 12 slices

For the cake

250g cooked beetroot
(not in vinegar or brine or
anything)
100g dark chocolate
(70% cocoa solids)
125g butter
150g dark muscovado sugar
150g light muscovado sugar
3 eggs, beaten
225g self-raising flour
30g cocoa powder
pinch of salt

To decorate

100g icing sugar
Red gel food colouring*
30g packet of Millions,
blackcurrant flavour

Preheat the oven to 180°C/350°F/gas 4 and grease and line a 23cm cake tin. Grate the beetroot and set aside.

Melt the chocolate using your favoured method (see page 20) and set that aside too. Cream the butter and sugars and gradually add the eggs. Sift the flour, cocoa powder and salt into the butter mix.

Stir in the beetroot, then the melted chocolate. Scrape the mix into the prepared tin and bake for 35 to 50 minutes. Do the Skewer Test (see page 23) and when you're happy, put the tin on a wire rack. When the cake is cool, take it out of the tin.

Make the icing by adding 1 tablespoon water to the icing sugar. If it's too thick, add a *little* more water, but go easy, you don't want it too runny. Add the red food colouring. Pour it over the top of the cake and let it run down the sides. Finally, scatter over the packet of Millions.

*I used Sugarflair's Ruby.

Orange and Cashew Cake

This is a fine, hefty cake, quite massive, and should feed several hundred people. I was slightly worried that the breadcrumbs might weight it down, but the egg whites counterbalance any possible heaviness and the addition of the orange syrup is a delightful, citrusy game changer.

Makes at least 20 slices

110g butter

170g caster sugar

3 eggs, separated

100g ground cashew nuts

90g breadcrumbs

125ml orange juice

1 teaspoon grated orange zest

300g plain flour

3 teaspoons baking powder

For the orange syrup

170g caster sugar

65ml orange juice

Preheat the oven to 180°C/350°F/gas 4 and liberally (wonderful word!) grease a 25cm bundt pan.

Cream together the butter, sugar and egg yolks. Add the ground cashew nuts, breadcrumbs, orange juice and orange zest. Sieve in the flour and baking powder and fold through. In a separate bowl, beat the egg whites until stiff, then fold gently into the mix.

Spoon the mix into the tin and bake for approximately 55 minutes, until the outside has gone lovely and crusty. Remove from the oven and put on a wire rack, but don't take the cake out of the tin! It needs to stay *in situ* until it absorbs the orange syrup.

Meanwhile, make the syrup by heating the sugar and orange juice gently. Stir until the sugar has dissolved. Prick the surface of the cake with a fork – lots and lots of times, but gently, you want to puncture, not fracture – then pour over the syrup and leave to infuse for as long as possible; overnight would be wonderful. Cut into slices and serve to multitudes (in reality, it makes about 20 slices).

Sweet Potato Pie

Exotic as this pie is, it's actually very simple to make. And you can make it super-simple if you use a shop-bought, pre-baked pastry case, but it must be at least 3cm deep to fit all the filling. If you decide to make your own pastry case and you're new to pastry, take a look at the Pastry section of this book (see page 112) before you go any further.

Serves 8

For the pastry

170g plain flour

pinch of salt

100g cold butter, cut into cubes

OR

1 x 20cm pre-baked shortcrust pastry case, at least 3cm deep

For the pie

625g sweet potatoes, peeled and cut into cubes

2 eggs

60g light brown soft sugar

3 tablespoons maple syrup

½ teaspoon ground cinnamon

½ teaspoon ground nutmeg

200ml double cream

To serve

shop-bought chocolate sauce in a squeezy bottle

If you're making your own pastry, sieve the flour and salt into a bowl, then add the cubed butter. Use the tips of your fingers to rub small pieces of butter and small pieces of flour together, until the mix begins to resemble fine breadcrumbs. Add a tablespoon or two of cold water if needed.

Refrigerate the pastry for an hour, then roll it out on to a floured surface. Preheat the oven to 180°C/350°F/gas 4, then liberally butter a 20cm pie tin or dish with a 3cm depth, and line it with the pastry.

Blind bake for 15 minutes, then remove from the oven and keep standing by.

In a large saucepan of water, bring the sweet potato cubes to a boil, then reduce to a simmer for about 15 minutes, until soft. Drain, then purée. You can do this by mashing or by using a food processor, but make sure it's *completely* smooth, with no dodgy lumps still hanging around. Leave to cool fully.

Preheat the oven to 190°C/375°F/gas 5. Put the pastry case on a baking tray.

Whisk the eggs, sugar and maple syrup, then add the puréed sweet potato, the cinnamon, nutmeg and cream. Pour into the pastry case.

Bake for approximately 40 to 50 minutes until almost set, but still with a slight wobble in the centre. Keep an eye on the pastry because as it's already baked, there's a chance the edges might burn. If they look like they might be going too dark, cover loosely with tinfoil.

Cool on a wire tray, then chill in the fridge for at least an hour. Just before serving, drizzle over the shop-bought chocolate sauce.

Chocolate Squash Tray Bake

Again, as with the beetroot cake, I beg of you to keep an open mind here. Certainly for me, the notion of using squash in a sweet cake was a challenging one, but my reservations lasted just as long as it took me to eat a slice. This really works, especially with the addition of the figs, which give a lovely sticky texture.

I've used a big baking tray so that the cake comes out quite shallow and flat. Don't be alarmed by this – it is dense and muscular enough to hold its own.

It would be perfectly acceptable to serve this cake plain and unadorned, but I've covered mine with a layer of chocolate ganache because I have difficulty with the concept of restraint.

Makes 21 fingers

100g squash, such as
  butternut

225g dark chocolate
  (70% cocoa solids)

175g butter

3 eggs

175g dark muscovado sugar

100g light muscovado sugar

250g plain flour

3 teaspoons baking powder

150g dried figs, chopped
  small

For the ganache

200g dark chocolate
  (70% cocoa solids)

100ml double cream

coloured chocolate vermicelli

Preheat the oven to 180°C/350°F/gas 4. Grease and line a 30cm by 23cm baking tin. Grate the squash and set aside.

Melt the chocolate and butter together in a heatproof bowl over a saucepan of hot water. In a separate bowl, beat the eggs with the sugars, then add the melted chocolate and butter. Stir in 275ml cold water, then sift in the flour and baking powder. Add the grated squash and chopped figs and mix well.

Pour into the prepared tray and bake for approx. 50 minutes. Do the Skewer Test (see page 23), then cool on a wire rack.

When the cake is fully cooled, prepare the chocolate ganache by melting the chocolate using your favoured method (see page 20) and stirring in the cream. Pour over the cake and scatter with chocolate vermicelli.

When this is set, it's time to cut the cake into fingers, each approximately 10cm by 3cm. Because this is such a big cake – 'unwieldy' you could say – it might be easier to do the cutting while the cake is still in the tin.

Tamarind, Date and Sour Cherry Muffins

Tamarind is my 'thing', the ingredient that I bandy around in conversations when I want to sound like I'm an adventurous and pioneering baker. 'Oh yes,' I say, striving to sound casual, 'I find that a teaspoon of tamarind gives a wonderfully intriguing sourness.' And then I say a little prayer and hope I get the chance to make a face of mock surprise and say, 'You don't know what tamarind is?! Well, I believe it's some sort of fruit, originally from Sudan, used a lot in Malaysian cooking, or so I'm told.'

Anyway, tamarind isn't half as exotic as it used to be. Time was you had to go to the Asian market – or indeed Malaysia itself – to get tamarind paste, but now it can be bought in my local supermarket.

The one thing about tamarind that remains as true as when I first began baking with it is that it really *does* give a wonderfully intriguing sourness – so sour, in fact, that I would strongly urge caution when it comes to licking the spoon after you've been dealing with it.

However, it works really well in this recipe. Itself and the cherries lead a spirited crusade of sourness, which is brought to heel by the powerful dark forces of the dates and the muscovado sugar. (Sorry about that sentence, I've been watching *Camelot*.)

Now, about 'muffins'. I'm not sure at what size cupcakes stop being cupcakes and officially become large enough to be called 'muffins'. I'm calling these little cakes 'muffins', but I'm worried about misleading you. As muffins go, they're probably at the smaller end of the scale, so if you'd prefer to call them 'cupcakes', then work away. I've decorated them with a simple glacé icing, coloured orange.

Makes 12

100g dried dates

100g dried sour cherries

125g butter

30g tamarind paste

2 eggs

75g dark muscovado sugar

140g plain flour

1 teaspoon bicarbonate of soda

For the icing

300g icing sugar

4 tablespoons water or lime juice

orange food colouring*

20g dried sour cherries

*I used Sugarflair's Tangerine/Apricot.

Preheat the oven to 180°C/350°F/gas 4 and line a 12-hole muffin (or cupcake) tin with paper cases.

Chop the dates and sour cherries very finely, then place in a saucepan with 150ml water and bring to the boil. Boil for 1 minute, then remove from the heat and add the butter. Stir until it has melted, then add the tamarind and leave to cool for maybe 10 minutes.

In a separate bowl, whisk the eggs and sugar. Add the cooled fruit/butter mix, then sieve in the flour and bicarbonate of soda and fold through. Don't worry if the sugar goes hard and lumpy, the lumps will dissolve during the baking time. Divide the mix among the paper cases and bake for about 15 to 17 minutes. Cool the tray on a wire rack.

Make the icing by gradually adding the water or lime juice to the icing sugar, until you've achieved your desired runniness. Then add the orange food colouring. Spoon the icing over the top of each muffin and use a knife to encourage it to the edges. Scatter the chopped cherries in a little heap in the centre. Practise saying the words, 'wonderfully intriguing sourness' in front of the mirror, then serve.

Mango Upside-Down Cake

A variation of the childhood favourite, Pineapple Upside-Down Cake. It is phenomenally easy to make.

Serves 6–8

For the topping

50g butter

50g light muscovado sugar

425g tin of sliced mango in syrup, drained (Reserve 2 tablespoons of the syrup.)

For the cake

100g butter

100g caster sugar

2 eggs

100g self-raising flour

1 teaspoon baking powder

Liberally grease a 20cm cake tin. This is actually one situation where I would counsel *against* using a loose-bottomed or springform tin because the first time I made this cake, I had 'leakage'. The juice from the mango made its way out through the gap in my tin and covered the base of the oven with a – frankly delicious – sort of caramel. Preheat the oven to 180°C/350°F/gas 4.

For the topping, beat the butter and sugar together, then spread it over the base of the cake tin – it will be a very thin layer, do not be alarmed. Then arrange the drained mango slices on top of the topping, in the most artistic way you can manage. Feel free to cut the slices up to plug any gaps.

Make the cake by creaming the butter and sugar together, adding the eggs and the 2 tablespoons of reserved mango syrup. Sieve in the flour and baking powder and fold through.

Spread the cake batter over the sliced mangoes, covering them, then bake for 35 minutes. Cool for 5 minutes – yes, only 5 minutes – on a wire rack then, trying not to burn your fingers, turn the cake out on to a serving plate. Serve warm, with a dollop of fresh cream.

Raspberry and Strawberry Upside-Down Cake

In a way, you might think I have a bit of a cheek, fobbing you off with this recipe, which is very, very similar to the Mango Upside-Down Cake I've just given you. But even though the cake part is – yes, I admit it – *identical*, the fruit is so different that this is an entirely different cake. Also, I've baked this cake in a heart-shaped tin and because the fruit here is red, it looks fantastic.

Serves 6–8

For the topping

50g butter

50g light muscovado sugar

425g tin of raspberries in juice, drained

425g tin of strawberries in juice, drained

(Reserve 2 tablespoons of the juice.)

For the cake

100g butter

100g caster sugar

100g self-raising flour

2 eggs

1 teaspoon baking powder

Liberally grease a heart-shaped tin (the one I used is about 23cm across at its widest point, and holds about a litre and a quarter of liquid). Preheat the oven to 180°C/350°F/gas 4.

For the topping, beat the butter and sugar together, then spread it over the base of the cake tin – it will be a very thin layer, do not be alarmed. Then arrange the drained berries on top of the topping, in the most artistic way you can manage.

Make the cake by creaming the butter and sugar together, adding the eggs and the 2 tablespoons of reserved berry juice. Sieve in the flour and baking powder and fold through.

Spread the cake batter over the berries, covering them, then bake for 35 minutes. Cool for 5 minutes on a wire rack then, trying not to burn your fingers, turn the cake out on to a serving plate. It will look fantastic. The only thing about heart-shaped cakes is that they're tricky to cut into slices that don't look peculiar. I can see no way round it, I'm sorry. Serve warm or cold, it's up to you.

Pear, Almond and Tahini Cake

Now *this* almost does count as healthy eating. It's dairy free – no butter or eggs – the fat is provided by the tahini. (I'm assuming you're familiar with tahini? It's a delicious paste made by crushing sesame seeds.) Also, this recipe has no sugar! I used date syrup, which I got in my local health food shop, but if you've trouble getting hold of it, you can use another syrup, for example, maple syrup.

Serves 12–14

240g tahini

260g date syrup

1 teaspoon bicarbonate of soda

220g plain flour

1 teaspoon ground cinnamon

100g almonds, chopped roughly

150g pears, peeled and diced into 2cm cubes*

250ml apple juice**

*You can even use canned if you haven't any fresh ones handy. I did.

**If you've decided to use canned pears, you can use the leftover pear juice. If it doesn't come to quite 250ml, top it up with apple juice.

Grease a 23cm cake tin and line the base with baking paper. Preheat the oven to 170°C/325°F/gas 3.

Give the tahini a quick stir while it's still in its jar, because the oil usually separates into a layer on the top. Then pour into a mixing bowl and beat with the date syrup. Add the bicarbonate of soda and mix again.

In a separate bowl, combine the sieved flour, cinnamon, almonds and diced pears. Add a third of the flour/nut mix to the tahini and mix. Add half the apple juice, then mix.

Add another third of the flour, then the other half of the juice. Finish with the remaining flour and mix until combined.

Pour the batter into the tin and bake for 45 minutes After 30 minutes drop the oven temperature to 160°C/325°F/gas 3 and cover the cake loosely with tinfoil for the final 10 minutes. Remove from the oven and let the cake cool in the tin. It is so rich and wonderful it doesn't need any sort of icing.

German Stollen Cake

This wonderful cake is traditionally served in Germany at Christmas time. It's fabulous, a sort of bread-like fruit cake, but with a hidden heart of marzipan. It involves the use of yeast, which used to scare the daylights out of me. Then I discovered dried instant yeast and it's changed my world.

I've read dozens of Stollen recipes, in the hope of making one as authentically German as possible, but there's such a wide variety of ingredients and methods that my head nearly exploded. I've experimented with a fair few versions and in the end, I decided on this recipe because it's quite easy and phenomenally delicious.

Makes 2 smallish, 25cm-long loaves, and you'll get about 10 slices out of each

50g currants

50g sultanas

50g raisins

100g glacé cherries, chopped

50g candied peel

4 tablespoons rum*

165ml full-fat milk

300g strong white bread flour

7g sachet of dried fast-action bread yeast

pinch of salt

75g butter, at room temperature

1 egg

55g caster sugar

250g marzipan**

To decorate

icing sugar

*If you're not happy using alcohol, orange juice will do instead.

**A quick note on marzipan. Some people make their own and good luck to them. I bought mine in Tesco's.

Soak the fruit in the rum, cover and set aside for at least a couple of hours. Overnight would be better.

When you're ready to start, heat the milk to lukewarm (no hotter or it'll kill the yeast) in a saucepan. In a separate bowl, sieve the flour, the yeast and the salt. Add the warm milk and mix well. You might see a few bubbles. This is an excellent sign, evidence that the yeast is working.

Add the butter, egg and sugar and mix again. Cover the bowl with a damp warm cloth and put in a warm place for about an hour and a half. You are leaving it to 'prove' – this is a breadmaking term, which means the yeast will do its magic and when you come back, the dough should have increased in volume, it might even have doubled, and will have developed a strange, elastic texture.

Turn the lump of dough (it will be quite sticky) out on to a floured work surface and 'knock it back'. This is *another* breadmaking term, which means, basically, that you punch all the air out of it and reduce it to its original size. Then put it back into the bowl, add in the soaked fruit and mix well.

If you're lucky enough to have a KitchenAid, use your dough hook to do the hard work and take a moment to give thanks. If you don't have a mixer, knead by hand on a well-floured surface for a good 5 minutes (sorry). At this point, line a baking tray with baking paper.

Take your marzipan, divide it in half and roll into two 'ropes', each about 20cm long. Take about half of the stollen dough out of the bowl. Place it on the floured surface and, using your hands, shape into a loaf about 22cm long and 9cm across. Place the marzipan rope down along the length of the loaf, in the middle, then fold in the sides of the stollen dough and squeeze them together, so that

•••

the marzipan is completely covered. Transfer the loaf to your prepared baking tray, seam side down.

Repeat the process for the second loaf, then cover the two loaves with a damp, warm cloth and leave to prove – yes, again – for about 40 minutes. (*Entre nous*, my loaves don't puff out and rise at all during this second 'proving', but still taste lovely. I don't know what to make of it.)

Preheat the oven to 180°C/350°F/gas 4 and bake the loaves for 10 minutes. Then lower the temperature to 150°C/300°F/gas 2 and bake for another 30 to 40 minutes, until the loaves look golden brown. Remove them from the baking tray, cool on a wire rack and sprinkle with icing sugar. (Do it through a sieve for a nice, even effect.)

Sweetcorn, Coconut and Lime Loaf

Sweetcorn. Yes, I know, strange for a cake. But the clue is in the name. *Sweet* corn. Not *savoury* corn. Or *sour* corn. *Sweet* corn. I had to fiddle around with this recipe a lot because even though it was delicious and sweet and texturally very interesting, it wouldn't rise. After a fair bit of experimentation, I concluded that the heaviness of the sweetcorn was responsible and I was in despair, my amigos, *despair*. I thought I'd just have to let this one go. Then, in a light-bulb moment, I hit on the notion of separating the eggs and beating the whites into a light, airy, cloud, then I let the battle commence. I pitted the sweetcorn against the beaten egg whites in a bare-knuckle fight – heaviness versus lightness. And guess what? Everyone's a winner!

Makes 12 slices

125g butter

125g caster sugar

3 eggs, separated

50g desiccated coconut

100g canned sweetcorn, drained

zest of 2 limes

125g self-raising flour

1 teaspoon baking powder

1 teaspoon bicarbonate of soda

Grease and line a 1 litre loaf tin (or use a silicone one, much easier) and preheat the oven to 190°C/375°F/gas 5.

Cream the butter and sugar until the mix goes pale. Add the egg yolks, desiccated coconut, sweetcorn kernels and lime zest and mix thoroughly. Sieve in the flour, baking powder and bicarbonate of soda and fold through.

In a separate bowl, whisk the egg whites until stiff then, using a large metal spoon, carefully fold into the other mixture.

Pile into your prepared tin and bake for approx. 30 minutes. Cool on a wire rack, then upend from the tin and cut into slices.

CHOCOLATE

Chocolate and Sour Cream Cake

Chestnut and Rum Brownies

Ultimate Chocolate Brownies

Sean's Rosemary Truffles

Rocky Road Cake

Black Forest Gateau Trifle

Balsamic, Black Pepper and Chocolate Cake

Quick-and-Easy Chocolate Fudge Pudding

Chocolate, Chilli and Cardamom Tart

Individual Chocolate Lava Cakes

Only an idiot would write a bakery book and not have a section on **CHOCOLATE**. That's all I can say. Therefore this chapter needs no introduction.

Chocolate and Sour Cream Cake

This is an excellent cake, very moist – thanks to the raspberries, I think – and surprisingly easy to make. Also, by using just raspberry jam to decorate, it keeps things very simple, if simple is what you're in the humour for.

Serves 12

100g dark chocolate
(70% cocoa solids)

250g self-raising flour

1 teaspoon bicarbonate of
soda

1 teaspoon salt

250g golden caster sugar

125ml sunflower oil

250ml sour cream

2 eggs, beaten

1 teaspoon vanilla extract

2 x 300g tins of raspberries,
drained of their juices*

To decorate

4–5 tablespoons raspberry
jam

*Or approx. 230g fresh
raspberries, but – perhaps
unexpectedly – I think the
tinned ones are better in
this case. Their pulpiness,
which in the real world
might be seen as a bad
thing, works very well
for this cake.

Oil two 23cm tins (you can use your hands or a piece of kitchen paper) and preheat the oven to 180°C/350°F/gas 4.

Melt the chocolate using your preferred method (see page 20) and leave to cool slightly.

Sieve the flour and bicarbonate of soda into a large mixing bowl. Add the salt and sugar, then stir in the oil and sour cream.

Mix in the melted chocolate.

Add in the beaten eggs, vanilla extract and 60ml hot water. Finally, stir through the raspberries.

Divide the mix between the two tins and bake for 25 minutes. Remove from the oven and set the tins on wire racks. Wait until the cakes are fully cooled before removing from their tins.

Sandwich the two layers together with raspberry jam.

Chestnut and Rum Brownies

Strange things, chestnuts, I find. Because, no matter how much bragging they do in their name, they don't *act* like nuts. Where's the crunch? Okay, *technically* they might be nuts, but texture-wise it's all a little unsettling. If I might speak frankly, they've a touch of the chickpea about them. But, handled right, they can be delicious.

There's both chestnut purée and actual chestnuts in this recipe and I hope you don't have trouble getting the chestnut purée – it comes in tins if that's any help.

I've used milk chocolate here and it gives a slightly milder, sweeter taste than the dark chocolate in the Ultimate Chocolate Brownies recipe. But overall, it's still very, very, very rich. It's really okay to cut this into sixteen pieces because even a small piece is very effective.

Finally, feel free to use real rum if you'd prefer it to the rum essence, but if you're doing that, put in 2 tablespoons instead of 2 capfuls.

Serves 9 or 16, depending on how generous you want to be

200g milk chocolate
100g butter
2 eggs
1 egg yolk
200g light muscovado sugar
200g chestnut purée
1 teaspoon vanilla extract
2 capfuls of rum essence
175g plain flour
½ teaspoon baking powder
100g chestnuts, roughly chopped

Liberally butter a 20cm square tin (loose-bottomed, if possible) and preheat the oven to 180°C/350°F/gas 4.

Melt the chocolate and butter together in a heatproof bowl over a saucepan of hot water.

In a separate bowl, beat the eggs, egg yolk and sugar together, then add the melted chocolate and butter.

Add the chestnut purée, the vanilla extract and the rum essence and mix well.

Sieve in the flour and baking powder and fold through.

Stir in the chestnuts until they're evenly distributed.

Pour the brownie mix into the prepared tin.

Bake for 30 minutes. It might look done on the top, but it won't be in the middle. Remember, this is a brownie, not a cake. Normal cake rules do not apply. Forget your Skewer Test! It has no place here.

Cool on a wire rack and leave for a long, long, long time (preferably overnight) before you cut it. It will be fabulously gooey and rich and wonderful.

Ultimate Chocolate Brownies

Yes, a second Brownies recipe! But this is quite different to the Chestnut and Rum Brownies – a lot darker. Very gooey, dense, sticky, chocolatey, wonderful.

Serves 9

225g dark chocolate
   (70% cocoa solids),
   roughly chopped
225g butter
2 eggs
2 egg yolks
200g light brown soft sugar
170g plain flour
½ teaspoon baking powder
pinch of salt
100g brazil nuts, chopped
   quite small

Liberally butter a 20cm square tin (loose-bottomed, if possible) and preheat the oven to 160°C/325°F/gas 3.

Gently melt the chocolate and the butter together in a heatproof bowl over a pan of hot water.

Beat the eggs, egg yolks and sugar together until they start to look a bit like caramel.

Pour in the melted chocolate and butter and mix together, but don't overbeat because if you do (I did on my first go) it sort of 'coagulates'. Not good.

Sieve in the flour, baking powder and salt and fold through.

Add the chopped brazil nuts and gently mix.

Pour into the prepared tin and bake for a mere 20 minutes. As with the Chestnut and Rum Brownies, normal cake rules don't apply here. We are in a strange foreign land where your trusty Skewer Test has no place.

Put the tin on a wire rack to cool for at least 3 hours. If you cut it too soon, the brownie will leak all over the place. (I make these mistakes so that you don't have to…) When the time is up, turn out of the tin and cut into nine equal-sized squares.

FYI, and this can be our little secret, the square in the middle will be the most delicious of them all. I'm only saying, for when you're dishing them out, if you wanted to single someone out for a special treat – and who's to say it can't be you? – then the middle one is the very, very best.

Sean's Rosemary Truffles

Sean is my sister Caitriona's husband and is one of the best cooks in the whole wide world. He is a genius. Fact. These truffles are an adaptation – an homage, if you will – of some chocolate rosemary ice cream he once made me. Eating that dessert was one of the most agonizing experiences I have ever had because I knew that at some stage it would end. I knew that the time would come when I had eaten my last mouthful and there would be no more, and frankly I didn't know how I would carry on.

The ice cream was – no word of a lie – amazing and I wanted to try – humbly, humbly, of course – to recreate Sean's recipe. However, I didn't have an ice cream maker so he suggested that, using the same basic ingredients, I make truffles instead. At first, this bamboozled me. 'Truffles?' I asked. 'Do you mean like the ones you get in a box? For your birthday? From an expensive chocolate shop?' 'The very ones,' he replied.

This was a complete revelation, that a person could make truffles in their own home. It was sort of like learning that I could knock up a pair of Christian Louboutin shoes in my utility room.

The ingredients are simple. The technique isn't too tricky either – I use a melon baller to make the roundy shapes. To decorate, I rolled the truffles in coloured sanding sugar, which added colour but no extra flavour. However, you could roll them in cocoa powder, desiccated coconut, ground pistachios, anything at all, which will, of course, change and enhance the flavour.

It's not necessary, but if you can get your hands on some mini paper cases to serve your truffles in, they will look extra beautiful.

Makes approx. 30–40

150ml double cream
8 sprigs of fresh rosemary
150g dark chocolate
  (70% cocoa solids)
25g butter

To decorate
coloured sanding sugar

Pour the cream into a saucepan.

Wash and dry the rosemary sprigs, then put 4 sprigs in the saucepan with the cream. Scald the cream (see page 21).

Remove the pan from the heat and let the rosemary flavour infuse the cream for about an hour.

Meanwhile, chop the chocolate very finely – use a food processor if it makes it easier – and place in a heatproof bowl. Dice the butter and add it to the chocolate.

Reheat the cream, then pour it through a sieve into the bowl of chocolate and butter. Discard the used rosemary sprigs.

Hopefully the heat of the cream will melt the chocolate and butter, but if it doesn't, please don't worry. Simply place the bowl over a saucepan of simmering water until everything is melted. Stir well to combine, remove from the heat, then lay the remaining 4 sprigs of rosemary along the surface. Don't immerse them deep in the mix because they are 'the very devil' (love that phrase) to remove – sprigs coming off, defiantly refusing to leave and all sorts of difficulties.

•••

Refrigerate for several hours, even overnight, if you like. The mix will set, but not become rock hard.

When you're ready to start making your truffles, take the mixture out of the fridge (you may need to let it warm a little before shaping), carefully peel off the sprigs of rosemary and discard them.

Pour coloured sanding sugar into a bowl.

Use your melon baller to scoop out a ball of the truffle mix, then drop it into the bowl of sanding sugar and roll it around a little until it's coated. Place it in a mini paper case. This will get easier with practice.

If you want, you can use the palms of your hands to encourage the truffles into roundy shapes, but bear in mind that this mix melts and gets messy very quickly and the heat of your hands might just accelerate the process.

Indeed, even without using your hands, you might need to put the chocolate mix back in the fridge periodically to firm it up again. But that's okay. Use the time in between to think pleasant thoughts. Like how impressed everyone will be when you present them with home-made truffles.

Rocky Road Cake

A no-bake cake. Easy peasy to make and everyone loves it.

Makes 16 squares

500g rich tea biscuits
300g dark chocolate
  (70% cocoa solids)
300g milk chocolate
200g butter
300g golden syrup
100g dried dates,
  chopped small
100g dried apricots,
  chopped small
120g hazelnuts, skins
  off, roasted and
  chopped roughly
100g mini marshmallows

I used ready roasted hazelnuts with their skins off, but if you prefer to roast your own: place the hazelnuts in a single layer on a baking tray and roast in a 180°C/350°F/gas 4 oven for 5 to 8 minutes or under the grill for 2 minutes until browned, checking regularly that they aren't burning.

To make the cake, begin by lining a 20cm square tin with clingfilm, leaving bits overhanging the sides so you can lift the cake out easily.

Break the biscuits into small pieces, smaller than bite-sized, but not reduced entirely to crumbs.

Melt the chocolate, butter and golden syrup in a large heatproof bowl set over a pan of simmering water.

Remove the bowl from the heat and stir in the broken biscuits, then add the dried fruit, nuts and marshmallows.

Stir well, then pour into the prepared tin and refrigerate for 6 hours.

Lift out of the tin and peel off the clingfilm. Cut into sixteen chunks. Watch people devour.

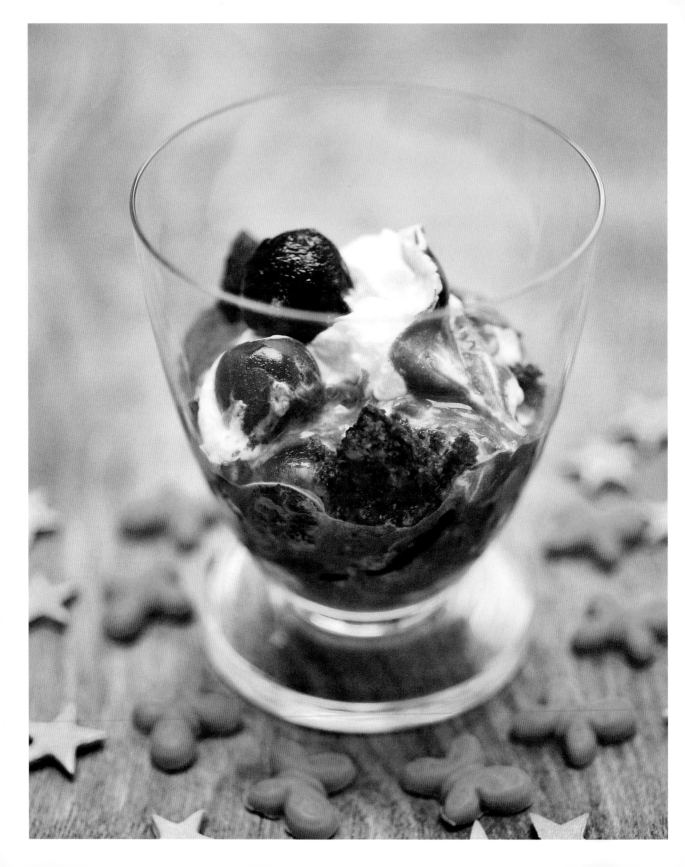

Black Forest Gateau Trifle

This is a variation on an old favourite, 'Ordinary Trifle'. Are you familiar with 'Ordinary Trifle'? Just in case you're not, it's a dessert traditionally made up of layers of strawberries, vanilla sponge, strawberry jelly, custard, whipped cream and more strawberries. But in keeping with the Black Forest theme, I'm using cherries, cherry jelly, chocolate sponge and chocolate custard.

The actual preparation time is short, but there are long, long, long gaps between each stage. It's best if you start on this the day before you plan on eating it.

Serves 8

2 x 400g tins of cherries, in syrup or juice – either is fine

135g packet of cherry jelly*

200g chocolate sponge**

For the custard

6 egg yolks

150g caster sugar

500ml pouring cream

200g dark chocolate (70% cocoa solids), chopped very finely

For the topping

150ml whipping cream

*If you can't get cherry, blackcurrant will do. Something dark coloured in any case.

**Or you could just buy a couple of chocolate muffins.

Drain one of the tins of cherries and put the juice to one side, perhaps on the windowsill, it's up to you really. Put the cherries in the bottom of a 2 litre bowl, preferably see-through, so that people can see your layers and admire them. Pack them down tight.

Make the jelly by dissolving the cubes in 100ml boiling water in a heatproof jug, then microwaving for a minute. Use the leftover juice to make it up to a half litre, then leave until it's *almost* set. *Almost* set, but not *fully* set. A fine line, but an important one. This will take hours and hours and hours. Longer if you're in a hurry. But bank on at least 3 hours.

When the jelly finally becomes thick and viscous, break the chocolate muffins into bite-sized pieces and put them into the bowl, on top of the cherries. Pour the jelly in on top. More setting will take place.

Meanwhile, make a start on the chocolate custard. In an entirely new and separate bowl, whisk the egg yolks with the sugar until thick and foamy. In a saucepan scald the cream (see page 21).

Add half a cup of the scalded cream to the egg yolks, whisking continuously. When it's fully incorporated, add another half cup and so on until all the cream is in.

Keep whisking and the mixture should thicken somewhat, then add in the chopped chocolate and stir until it's melted.

Set aside to cool fully. And when I say 'fully', I mean 'fully' because if you pour the custard in on top of the jelly when it's still even a little bit hot, it will melt the jelly and the whole thing will be a shambles. A shambles, I tell you. (Christ, now that I think about it, making trifle has been one of the most stressful events of my life …)

So yes, pour the fully cooled custard on top of the jelly and leave aside to set – at least an hour.

Just before serving, whip the cream and spread it over the chocolate custard. Drain the second can of cherries – you can do what you like with the juice this time – and dot the cherries over the cream so that it looks like something out of a cartoon.

Balsamic, Black Pepper and Chocolate Cake

This is an adaptation of a recipe from the (very divine!) *Divine Chocolate* recipe book. I came across it when I was just back from a family holiday in Tuscany and was jonesing for some Italian produce.

This is a handy little cake because it's egg- and dairy-free and astonishingly easy to make. Please don't be scared off by the balsamic syrup and black pepper – they give an interesting and slightly odd undertow, but don't overpower things. However, I suggest serving this cake with mascarpone cheese and (this is where I might lose you) fresh basil and balsamic syrup. Think of sunny days in Italy is all I can say, and be grateful that at least I'm not advocating anchovies.

Serves 9, or 16 if you're feeling a bit mingy

175g plain flour
1 teaspoon baking powder
50g cocoa powder
175g light muscovado sugar
pinch of salt
½ teaspoon freshly ground
  black pepper
125ml walnut oil
1 tablespoon balsamic syrup
1 teaspoon white wine
  vinegar

To serve

250g tub of mascarpone
  cheese
a handful of finely torn fresh
  basil leaves*
a squeeze of balsamic syrup

*Go on! Go mad!

Oil a loose-bottomed 20cm square cake tin and preheat the oven to 180°C/350°F/gas 4.

Sieve the flour, baking powder and cocoa powder into a large mixing bowl. Add the sugar, salt and black pepper.

Stir in the oil, balsamic syrup, white wine vinegar and 150ml warm water and mix well.

Pour into the tin and bake for about 30 minutes.

Please note: this will be quite a 'flat' cake. It won't rise lots and there's only one layer. By itself, it won't look that impressive. I'm telling you now, so that you won't be disappointed. And so that you'll understand that what you serve it with is almost as important as the cake itself.

Cool on a wire rack.

When it's cold, remove from the tin and cut into nine squares. Or sixteen.

Serve with a dollop of mascarpone cheese. And the basil leaves and balsamic syrup, if you're feeling daring, but if you're not, don't worry, it will still be wonderful.

Quick-and-Easy Chocolate Fudge Pudding

This has an awful lot going for it, not least the fact that the chocolate taste is created by cocoa powder and not by chocolate itself, so there's a chance that there might be some cocoa powder in the house, unlike actual chocolate, which does not survive my regular 'sweeps' (I mean, I eat it). Also, everything goes in together, at the same time – the sponge, the sauce, the lot. You just fling it in and forget about it for 40 minutes.

And it tastes great. The sponge is light and chocolatey and the sauce is gooey and fudgey. Just one thing about the size of the dish you use. Make sure it has a capacity of at least 1.5 litres and is about 5cm deep. This might seem big and deep, but the first couple of times I made this pudding, I used a 1 litre dish and the topping 'burst its banks' and spattered itself over the inside of the oven. Poor Himself had a terrible job cleaning up after it.

Serves 6

For the sponge
115g light brown soft sugar
115g unsalted butter
1 teaspoon vanilla extract
2 eggs, lightly beaten
85g self-raising flour
30g cocoa powder
pinch of salt

For the sauce
85g dark muscovado sugar
30g cocoa powder
225ml milk

Butter a 1.5 litre ovenproof dish. Preheat the oven to 180°C/350°F/gas 4.

Cream together the sugar and butter until light and fluffy.

Beat in the vanilla extract and the eggs.

Sieve in the flour, cocoa powder and salt and fold through.

Spoon into the buttered ovenproof dish.

For the sauce, simply mix the sugar and the cocoa powder together and gradually whisk in the milk.

Pour evenly over the uncooked cake mixture – yes, I know it sounds odd, but it works.

Cover the dish loosely with a sheet of tinfoil and bake for about 45 minutes.

Serve hot, warm or cold, with or without cream.

Chocolate, Chilli and Cardamom Tart

This adaptation of a Lucas Hollweg recipe sounds – and tastes – very exotic, but is surprisingly easy to make. Especially because I'm giving you the super-easy option and encouraging you to use a shop-bought shortcrust pastry case. A 20cm would be ideal, and it needs to be only 1.5cm or 2 cm deep. But if you'd prefer to make your own pastry, see the recipes in the Pastry chapter (page 112).

I've just used one chilli here, which gives a hint of heat, a mere *soupçon*, if you will. If you'd prefer it to be hotter, add another chilli, even two. But leave out the seeds. Even though they're the hottest part of the chilli, for some reason they just become burny and nasty in this recipe.

Serves 6–8

1 x 20cm pre-baked
  shortcrust pastry case

For the filling
1 red chilli
9 cardamom pods
250ml double cream
50g caster sugar
250g dark chocolate
  (70% cocoa solids),
  broken into small pieces
70g butter, cut into small
  cubes

To decorate (optional)
edible gold leaf

For the filling, chop the chilli finely and discard the seeds. Rough up the cardamom pods by whizzing them in a coffee grinder, or flattening them with the blade of a wide knife and then chopping them as though they have insulted your mother.

Put the cream, sugar, cardamom pods and chopped chilli into a saucepan and gently bring to a simmer. Stir and heat until the sugar has dissolved, but be careful not to burn it.

Turn off the heat and leave to infuse for about an hour.

After an hour, reheat the cream mixture until it's just simmering, then put the chocolate and butter in a heatproof bowl and strain the warm cream on to it through a sieve, leaving the cardamom and chilli behind.

Hopefully the heat of the cream will melt the chocolate and butter, in which case, stir until the mixture is smooth and glossy.

However, sometimes when I've made this, the heat of the cream simply isn't enough to melt the chocolate. If that happens, don't panic. Simply put the bowl over a saucepan of simmering water and stir until the chocolate dissolves and the whole mix thickens up.

Pour it into the pastry case and decide whether you're serving this to six or eight people. Place a piece of edible gold leaf in the middle of each 'slice'. This is a fiddly business, as gold leaf is floaty and sticks to everything, including itself. You might have to use kitchen tweezers (which are exactly like ordinary tweezers, except they live in my kitchen and are only used on food).

Leave to cool for a few hours at room temperature. The combination of cream, chocolate and butter will set into a beautiful, almost fudgey texture, so wonderful that when you serve this tart to others, you might be met with jealousy. Rise above it.

Individual Chocolate Lava Cakes

The effort-to-effect ratio of these cakes is stunningly low. They're unbelievably simple to make (so simple that it actually made me uneasy, it made me wonder what I was doing wrong), yet they look and taste like something you'd pay good money for in a French restaurant. Especially if you manage to get them out of the ramekins (I'll come to that). These lava cakes are, in essence, warm chocolate cakes with a liquid chocolate centre. The idea is that you cut the cake open and the molten chocolate rushes out. You get to decide how liquid they are by the length of time you bake them for.

Serves 4

170g chocolate
 (70% cocoa solids)
170g butter, cut into cubes
3 eggs
85g caster sugar
85g plain flour

To serve
thinly sliced strawberries
squirty cream or vanilla
 ice cream

Get four 250ml ramekins and butter the living daylights out of them. I really mean it. If you're planning on turning these little delights on to plates, the ramekins need to be larded with butter.

Preheat the oven to 180°C/350°F/gas 4.

Melt the chocolate in a heatproof bowl over a saucepan of simmering water. Add the diced butter and stir until it melts.

In a separate bowl, beat the eggs and sugar until the mix goes pale and foamy. Stir in the melted chocolate.

Sieve in the flour and fold it through.

Divide the chocolate batter equally among the four buttered ramekins.

Cook for about 10 minutes if you want the cakes to be very runny; 12 minutes if you'd like them to be a little firmer. But I wouldn't leave them for much longer than 17 to 18 minutes.

At this stage, you can make life easy for yourself and simply sling the ramekins on to plates and throw on a dollop of vanilla ice cream. Or – painful gulp and squaring of shoulders – you could try taking the cakes out of the ramekins.

To do this, first stand the ramekins on a cold surface for about 5 minutes. The cakes will shrink a tiny bit – this is good, this gives you room to very carefully slide a small sharp knife in between the cake and the container.

Use the knife to gently loosen the connection between the two and when you feel you can do no more, tip a ramekin upside down on to a dessert plate, give it an encouraging little shake and keep your fingers crossed that the cake will come out without a fight.

Even if it all goes a bit disastrous, with the base of the cake defiantly refusing to let go of the ramekin, remove it with a spoon, reattach it to the main body of the cake and disguise the damage with a squirt of fake squirty cream or a dollop of vanilla ice cream.

Serve with thinly sliced strawberries and the aforementioned squirty cream or vanilla ice cream.

Index

Cassandra hurried to the connecting door. She had never opened it before, never gone to his side. She grasped the knob, then pressed her ear to the panel. Perhaps the nightmare was over.

Again the anguished sound followed by a terrible groan.

She pushed open the door to find him tottering to his feet. His eyes were open, his arms sawing the air wildly. She ran to him, caught him by the arm, but he shrugged her off.

Again the groan. "Coming!" he called. "Coming!"

Light was just breaking through the windows, dim yet enough for her to see. She waved her hand in front of his eyes. He did not blink.

"Edward," she whispered.

He took a tottering step. His free hand batted the air. "Coming!"

"This way." She managed to turn him and guide him around the bed. Once on the other side, she pushed him back, but he resisted her efforts, still struggling in the grip of his nightmare. "You're tired now," she soothed, stroking his shoulder and chest. "You're so tired. Lie down and rest."

At last with a deep sigh, he closed his eyes and sank back on the bed.

She worked the covers out from under his heavy limp body. They were twisted every which way with a great rent down one side of the top sheet. His nightmare had been terrifying indeed.

Now his breathing was even. Nevertheless, as she worked over him, he occasionally gave a faint sigh. The horrid dream still crouched at the edge of his consciousness.